Resource Governance and Protracted Conflict in Nigeria's Niger Delta

Conflict and Security in the Developing World

Series Editor: Akanmu G. Adebayo

Since the end of World War II, there have been more intrastate than interstate conflicts—and most of the violent conflicts have occurred in the developing world. Many conflicts are over complex issues of governance and development while others have been over ethnicity, politics, religion, and other cultural issues. They have often resulted in fragile, uncoordinated, failing or collapsed states, and grave global security concerns prompting massive peacekeeping, peacebuilding, and other conflict transformation efforts. This series publishes works that expand our understanding of, and that propose possible solutions to, issues of conflicts and security in the developing world. The series conceives the "developing world" broadly as transitional societies and emerging markets in Africa, Asia, Latin America, the Caribbean, and Oceania. The series publishes works that are interdisciplinary and cross-cutting, that combine Western and local perspectives, and that employ a diversity of research methods, theories, and approaches. Examples of topics include youth vulnerability and exclusion, police and policing, terrorism, small arms, genocidal wars, drug and human trafficking, security sector reform, natural resource governance, faith and violence, democratization and governance, gender and development, regional organizations and peacebuilding, electoral issues, and indigenous conflict management mechanisms. These works may cut across the region or focus on a country or community.

Recent Titles

Resource Governance and Protracted Conflict in Nigeria's Niger Delta: Understanding the Perceptions and Grievances of the People in Oil-Bearing Communities, by John B. Idamkue

Fighting in God's Name: Religion and Conflict in Local-Global Perspectives, edited by Afe Adogame, Olufunke Adeboye, and Corey L. Williams

Atone: Religion, Conflict, and Reconciliation, edited by Brandon D. Lundy, Akanmu G. Adebayo, and Sherrill W. Hayes

Nationalism and Intra-State Conflict in the Postcolonial World, edited by Michael Fonkem

Africa Nation in Peace Operations: Ghana Armed Forces in Lebanon and Liberia, by Emmanuel Wekem Kotia

Indigenous Conflict Management Strategies in West Africa: Beyond Right and Wrong, edited by Akanmu G. Adebayo, Brandon D. Lundy, Jesse J. Benjamin, and Joseph Kingsley Adjei

Resource Governance and Protracted Conflict in Nigeria's Niger Delta

Understanding the Perceptions and Grievances of the People in Oil-Bearing Communities

John B. Idamkue

LEXINGTON BOOKS
Lanham • Boulder • New York • London

Published by Lexington Books
An imprint of The Rowman & Littlefield Publishing Group, Inc.
4501 Forbes Boulevard, Suite 200, Lanham, Maryland 20706
www.rowman.com

6 Tinworth Street, London SE11 5AL, United Kingdom

British Library Cataloguing in Publication Information Available

Library of Congress Cataloging-in-Publication Data

Names: Idamkue, John B., 1960- author.
Title: Resource governance and protracted conflict in Nigeria's Niger Delta : understanding the perceptions and grievances of the people in oil-bearing communities / John B. Idamkue.
Description: Lanham : Lexington Books, [2021] | Series: Conflict and security in the developing world | Includes bibliographical references and index. | Summary: "This book identifies six pillars of resource governance to provide a nuanced understanding of the perceptions and grievances of the oil-bearing communities in Nigeria's Niger Delta. John B. Idamkue argues that resource governance is both at the heart of resource conflicts in the Niger Delta and the ideal place to find solutions"— Provided by publisher.
Identifiers: LCCN 2021004081 (print) | LCCN 2021004082 (ebook) | ISBN 9781793634801 (cloth) | ISBN 9781793634818 (epub)
Subjects: LCSH: Natural resources—Nigeria—Management. | Natural resources—Government policy—Nigeria.
Classification: LCC HC1055.Z65 I33 2021 (print) | LCC HC1055.Z65 (ebook) | DDC 333.709669/4—dc23
LC record available at https://lccn.loc.gov/2021004081
LC ebook record available at https://lccn.loc.gov/2021004082

Contents

List of Figures and Tables

FIGURES

TABLES

Acknowledgments

I wish to thank my Dissertation Committee, Dr. Akanmu Adebayo (Chair), Dr. Charity Butcher, and Dr. Brandon Lundy, for their suggestions, feedback, and invaluable guidance during my research. Dr. Adebayo kept me focused and provided tremendous mentorship including when I encountered challenges at my place of employment and in the family. Dr. Adebayo's bird's-eye view of Nigeria ensured that I had to get my facts right or else! Dr. Butcher's input improved my final product by emphasizing the connections in my study. Dr. Lundy's keen observations during the mapping stage of my study led me to a nuanced perspective on resource governance.

I am also grateful to Dr. Adebayo and Dr. Nurudeen Akinyemi for granting me graduate assistantships in the Center for Conflict Management and the Division of Global Affairs, respectively, at KSU. I acknowledge the assistance of Dr. Olutayo Adesina of the University of Ibadan, Nigeria, who kindly gave me an official invitation to conduct research in Nigeria in fulfillment of the KSU research requirement.

During my fieldwork, I benefited from the assistance of Patrick Naagbanton and Dr. Neninbarini Zabbey of the Center for Environment, Human Rights, and Development, Port Harcourt, Rivers State, Nigeria. I appreciate the moral encouragement of KSU alumni, Drs. Edoh Agbehonou, Chux Ibekwe, and Maureen Kperogi, throughout my journey.

Finally, I wish to thank members of my family for their love and immeasurable support—my wife Blessing, my daughter Regina (Koko), and my son David. Words cannot express my gratitude to you for holding down the home front while I took a long academic trip. I promise to make up for the time I was gone.

Abbreviations and Acronyms

All Progressives Congress (APC)
Armed Conflict Location and Event Data Project (ACLED)
Calabar, Ogoja, and Rivers State Movement (COR State Movement)
Central Bank of Nigeria (CBN)
Civil Liberties Organization (CLO)
Civil Society Organization (CSO)
Community-based organization (CBO)
Fund for Peace (FFP)
Ibrahim Index of African Governance (IIAG)
Ijaw Youth Council (IYC)
Institutional Review Board (IRB)
International oil companies (IOCs)
Joint Venture (JV)
Local Government Area (LGA)
Movement for the Emancipation of the Niger Delta (MEND)
Movement for the Survival of the Ogoni People (MOSOP)
National Liberation Army (ELN)
National Council of Nigeria Citizens (NCNC)
Nigeria Extractive Industries Transparent Initiative (NEITI)
Niger Delta Avengers (NDA)
Niger Delta Basin Development Board (NDBDB)
Niger Delta Development Commission (NDDC)
Niger Delta Peoples Volunteer Force (NDPVF)
Niger Delta Red Squad (NDRS)
Nigerian Institute of International Affairs (NIIA)
Nigerian National Petroleum Company (NNPC)
Non-governmental organization (NGO)

Ogoni Bill of Rights (OBR)
Organization of Petroleum Exporting Countries (OPEC)
Petroleum Industry Governance Bill (PIGB)
Protracted Social Conflict (PSC)
Revenue Mobilization Allocation and Fiscal Commission (RMAFC)
Shell Petroleum Development Company (SPDC)
United Nations Environment Program (UNEP)
United Nations Development Program (UNDP)

Chapter 1

The People Arose

The Genesis of the Conflict

Natural resource conflicts are clearly top of the list of intense and perennial conflicts within the Nigerian federation. In 2012, Nigeria earned 82 percent of its revenue and 90 percent of its foreign exchange from crude oil sales (Edame & Effiong, 2013). This study focuses on conflicts associated with crude oil production and the distribution of proceeds from petroleum rents, royalties, and taxes among the constituent units of the Nigerian federation. Why have the conflicts lingered for decades? What are the factors behind the resurgence of militant groups like the Niger Delta Avengers (NDA), several years after the introduction of the amnesty program? This study critically explores and seeks answers to these questions.

My interest in this study goes beyond the need to fulfill a requirement for my PhD degree. Born and raised in Nigeria, my life story intersects with the struggle over natural resources. I was a community organizer in the Ogoni area of Nigeria's Niger Delta region and a member of the Movement for the Survival of the Ogoni People (MOSOP), a community organization founded by writer Ken Saro-Wiwa to campaign for social and environmental justice for oil-producing communities. I was one of the young activists who helped Saro-Wiwa organize the historic Ogoni day protest against Shell Oil in 1993. Protests at this time were peaceful, but the repressive responses of the federal government of Nigeria forced many Ogoni people, including myself, into exile.

While conflicts associated with natural resources in the Federal Republic of Nigeria began in the 1990s, they reached their peak in 2005 and have lingered unabated ever since. Nigeria is a multiethnic, multilingual country rich in diversity of peoples, social groups, history, terrain, culture, and traditions (Umejesi, 2012). British colonial rule (1861–1960) amalgamated and corralled a multiplicity of diverse indigenous populations, hitherto separate, independent, fiercely competitive, self-sufficient political and economic entities, into one edifice. Nigeria is composed of majority and minority ethnic groups. The majority groups are the Hausa-Fulani in the north, the Igbo in the southeast, and the Yoruba in the southwest. These three groups constitute more than half of the country's population with the remaining divided among over 200 minority ethnic groups (Obasi & Otobo, 2011).

Observers and commentators expect that the success of Nigeria will serve as a beacon to other African countries. In 2015, for example, the successful conduct of the presidential election and the peaceful transfer of power to the opposition, for the first time, were celebrated the world over. Hopes were raised that Nigeria's example would rub off on other multicultural African countries. Some scholars believe Nigeria has not taken her rightful place in the comity of nations despite the abundance of human and natural resources (Isumonah, 2015; Moruku, 2012; Omeje, 2005; Osaghae, 2008). Yet others posit that the country has fared relatively well, given the challenges of state building in its sixty years of nationhood (Babalola, 2015; Ojo, 2010; Suberu, 2010).

Nigeria is an oil-producing country. Unlike other oil-producing countries in the Middle East that are religiously monolithic, Nigeria boasts of multiple religious traditions—African traditional religious practitioners, Christianity, and Islam. Significantly, the ethnic heterogeneity, religious differences, and cultural diversity make Nigeria prone to tensions and outbreak of hostilities and violent ethnic clashes (Adegbami, 2013; Oladeji, 2015; Omotoso, 2010; Orogun, 2010; Watts, 2015). Some other scholars hold a contrary view and posit that Nigeria's ethnic heterogeneity, religious plurality, and cultural diversity are indeed sources of national strength and stability (Babalola, 2015; Ojo, 2010; Suberu, 2010).

Nigeria is a unique federation. Nigeria's federal system of government has its origin in British colonialism (Adebayo, 1993). Initially governed as a unitary system from 1914, the colonial administration introduced the federal system through "devolution," in 1946, created regional governments, and introduced a federal constitution in 1954. After independence, the devolution of power by the federal government continued through the creation of more states, but the new states were much smaller and weaker than the old regional governments. Moreover, the country experienced a civil war in 1967–1970 and was governed by military heads of state for most of the next three decades.

Nigeria is a paradox that compels a robust scrutiny. Nigeria is blessed with abundant natural resources, particularly oil and gas deposits, a vibrant population, and good climate. Nigeria is the largest producer of crude oil in Sub-Saharan Africa and eighth in the world, and a member of the Organization of Petroleum Exporting Countries (OPEC) (CIA Fact Book, 2017). Yet the country lacks basic social infrastructure like stable electricity, pipe-born water, and health facilities. Indeed, the states that produce the petroleum (known collectively as the Niger Delta) are also among the least developed parts of Nigeria.

Poverty is widespread in the Niger Delta region, worsened by an exceptionally high cost of living created by the petro-economy. A 2006 United Nations Development Program Niger Delta Human Development Report (2006) concludes that the Niger Delta has "an appalling human development situation summed up in social instability, poor local governance, neglect of infrastructure, lack of access to fundamental services, environmental degradation, and extreme economic deprivation" (pp.15–16).

In the mid-1990s, grievances and protests against perceived unfair oil resource allocation started peacefully among a handful of communities in the southern part of the country. Within a decade, it took violent dimensions in response to alleged crackdown by the Nigerian military. Kidnappings of local and expatriate oil workers for ransom, takeovers of oil platforms, and invasion of oil fields and flow stations by armed youths became rampant. These escalated to violent agitations, insurrection, militancy, smuggling, and unauthorized drilling and the sale of crude oil by armed youths. Although I left Nigeria for several years, I continued to be personally and professionally interested in understanding how the character and environment of conflicts have changed over the years, what the perceptions of the stakeholders are about the sharing of proceeds from oil resources, and the impact of the conflicts on the livelihood of the local communities.

HOW IT ALL STARTED

In the early 1990s, Nigeria witnessed grievances and community protests mostly emanating from oil-producing communities in the Niger Delta region. Whereas commercial oil production started in full swing in the late 1950s, resource conflicts did not manifest on a large-scale until the mid-1990s, when they took a violent turn following the hanging of the indigenous rights activist, Ken Saro-Wiwa, by the military government of General Sani Abacha. Saro-Wiwa had formed MOSOP in 1990 and had begun to mobilize his people to protest government policy and operational practices of the oil companies, which, he claimed, polluted their environment, marginalized the people, and denied them their natural rights to the resources in the land (Watts, 2015).

Movement for the Survival of the Ogoni People (MOSOP) is a sociocultural umbrella organization of constituent associations of youth, women, churches, students, teachers, and professionals. Adopting nonviolent and peaceful methods, MOSOP launched an intensive campaign against the international oil companies (IOCs) operating in the Ogoni territory and the federal government of Nigeria. MOSOP activists accused the IOCs, particularly Shell Oil and Chevron, of polluting their farmlands and rivers through oil spills and gas flares. MOSOP also accused the government of "political marginalization" and argued that despite the huge revenue derived from crude oil production since 1958, estimated at $30 billion, the people of Ogoni had little or no benefits to show for it. It demanded local autonomy, a fair share of the resources exploited in their territory, and the end to environmental pollution (Saro-Wiwa, 1992, 1995).

Several other protest movements also emerged to articulate the grievances of these communities. Several researchers have studied the Niger Delta movements from multiple perspectives. Many studies have assessed the Niger Delta self-determination claims (Ejobowah, 2000; Omotola, 2009; Osaghae, 2008; Senewo, 2015) while other studies examined human rights violations and violence against the oil-producing communities (Frynas, 2001; Manby, 1999; Moruku, 2012; Okoro, 2009). Ako and Okonmah (2009), Umukoro (2012), and Orogun (2010) highlight environmental problems associated with oil production, while others analyzed the rise and growth of militant insurgency (Human Rights Watch, 2005; Ikelegbe, 2010; International Crisis Group, 2006). These studies, however, do not address the protracted and enduring character of the conflicts between the local communities, the transnational oil corporations, and the federal government. My study fills an important gap by investigating the resurgence of the conflicts and emergence of new actors, particularly youthful, militant ones.

Oil was first discovered in Oloibiri in present-day Bayelsa State in 1956 by Shell Darcy. The first shipment of oil export by Nigeria was shipped from the Bomu oil fields in Ogoni territory in Rivers State in 1958. Oil production has been the mainstay of the Nigerian economy since the early 1970s. Crude oil production is dominated by IOCs who enter into joint production agreements with the federal government-owned Nigerian National Petroleum Corporation (NNPC). Most of Nigeria's crude oil and gas deposits are found in the Niger Delta region in the southeast, inhabited by ethnic minorities who complain of marginalization in the distribution of revenue derived from oil exploration.

The severity, intensity, and longevity of resource conflicts in the Niger Delta compel incisive examination. The Uppsala Conflict Data Program, Human Rights Watch, Amnesty International, and Civil Liberties Organization (CLO) have given figures of deaths, detentions, arrests and displaced persons, refugees, and other victims since the conflict began. Estimates of resource conflict deaths averaged 1,500 per year from 2006 to 2012 and 100,000 persons were internally displaced (Watts, 2015). Nigeria's oil production fell to 1.5 million barrels a day from 2.5 million a day between January 2008 and

May 2009 due to the attacks by the Movement for the Emancipation of the Niger Delta (MEND), a decline of about 40 percent. In addition, by mid-July 2009, 124 of Nigeria's 252 active oil fields were shut down due to the activities of MEND. In the last quarter of 2008, a report prepared by a 43-member government panel entitled *The Report of the Technical Committee on the Niger Delta*, found that the Nigerian government lost a whopping $23.7 billion in oil revenues due to attacks by militants and sabotage in the first nine months of 2008 (Ihonvbere, 2009).

The Human Rights Committee of MOSOP alleged that 2,200 Ogonis were killed by security forces due to the conflict with the government and the oil companies in 1994 (MOSOP, 2001). Thousands of Ogoni refugees fled Nigeria to neighboring countries of Benin, Togo, and Ghana following the hanging of Saro-Wiwa and eight Ogoni activists in 1995. The United Nations High Commission for Refugees resettled well over 5,000 Ogoni refugees in the United States and Canada between 1996 and 2010 (MOSOP-USA, 2006).

A recurrent point by activists of the Niger Delta region is the contention that whereas the oil and gas resources are in their region, those who control and make decisions about the resources; for example, the allocations of oil blocks, oil mining licenses, and oil contracts, are usually from the north or some other part of the country. Moses Siasia, a governorship candidate in the 2015 elections in Bayelsa State, in a press statement on behalf of Niger Delta Young Leaders Stakeholders, warned that there would be no oil blocks to allocate or explore if Nigeria is not restructured (Kumolu, 2017). "Restructuring" has become a metaphor for splitting up the country into separate and independent countries.

Both the military government and the civilian administrations have responded to the agitations of the Niger Delta people in differing ways. The General Ibrahim Babangida regime (1985–1993) enacted the treasonable felony decree targeting Saro-Wiwa and his MOSOP campaign in 1993. The draconian edict prescribed the death penalty for anyone advocating ethnic autonomy in Nigeria and anyone who utters or publishes words suggesting the breakup of Nigeria, flies a flag, or suggests the creation of a new state or local government for the country (Ibeanu, 2000). The regime of General Sani Abacha (1993–1998) is alleged to have conducted high-handed and repressive raids in Ogoni territory and killed off scores of Ogoni indigenes in an attempt to scuttle their struggle (Frynas, 2001; Human Rights Watch, 1995; Ibeanu, 2000; Manby, 1999; Okoro, 2009; Pegg, 1999). The Abacha government eventually hung Saro-Wiwa and eight other Ogoni leaders in November 1995 and stationed thousands of soldiers, police, and other security forces in Ogoniland to prevent any further protests against his government.

While the civilian administration of President Olusegun Obasanjo (1999–2007) established the Niger Delta Development Commission (NDDC) to tackle the development problems of the region, his government was considered infamous for deploying Nigerian soldiers to overrun Odi in Bayelsa State, for some elements in that community were alleged to have killed some police officers. Obasanjo also introduced policy measures to deny the oil-producing states access to oil royalties from offshore oil fields. This move was vehemently opposed by the oil-producing states whose governments went to court to challenge the constitutional authority of a sitting president to usurp the rights of states to royalties and mining rents from offshore oil fields.

In 2009, a ceasefire agreement was signed between several Niger Delta militant organizations and the government. In addition, owing to the death of the substantive President Umaru Musa Yar'Adua in 2010, Vice President Goodluck Jonathan, who was a minority from the Ijaw ethnic group in the Niger Delta, became the President of Nigeria. Some observers have wondered if these events may possibly have contributed to fluctuations in the violent attacks on oil installations (Watts, 2015). Yet, the situation in the Niger Delta remains volatile as attacks on oil installations persist even into the Buhari presidency.

The Fund for Peace (FFP) reports that during the first six months of 2016, conflict-related incidents, violence, and fatalities have been on the increase in the Niger Delta region and were even higher than the last wave of militancy in 2009. The key oil-producing states of Bayelsa, Delta, and Rivers have recorded the highest per capita fatalities and witnessed a resurgence of militant groups, who have launched a series of attacks on energy infrastructure. Fatalities rose from 220 during the same period in 2015 to 400 in 2016 (Fund for Peace, 2016). Using statistics provided by Nigeria Watch, and Armed Conflict Location and Event Data (ACLED), FFP did a comparative analysis of fatalities resulting from the Boko Haram insurgency in the North East of Nigeria and the Niger Delta states' militancy. The study found that more conflict-related fatalities occurred in the Niger Delta during second quarter of 2016—450 deaths—compared to fifty deaths in the North East.

A new militant group, the NDA, emerged in February 2016 with a series of attacks on major oil pipelines in Delta and Bayelsa states. In addition to the well-known militant organizations such as MEND and the Niger Delta Peoples Volunteer Force (NDPVF), new and splinter groups have emerged in the Niger Delta since President Muhammadu Buhari won the election as Nigeria's president in 2015. The key militant groups in the Niger Delta include Red Egbesu Water Lions (REWL), New Delta Suicide Squad, Isoko Liberation Movement, Joint Niger Delta Liberation Force, Ultimate Warriors of Niger Delta, Niger Delta Red Squad (NDRS), and Egbesu Mightier Fraternity (Fund for Peace, 2016).

The Presidential Amnesty Program that provides stipends, skills training, and other benefits to ex-militants was introduced by President Umaru Yar'Adua in 2009 and later maintained by President Jonathan, who took over the presidency following the death of Yar'Adua, was to be phased out by the current government of President Buhari in 2018. Due to pressure from the ex-militants, Buhari shelved his plan to end the program. President Buhari's administration's cancellation of key security contracts held by ex-militant generals including Government Ekpemupolo AKA Tompolo and the stepping up of military operations in the creeks against the militants are said to have led to resumption of attacks by Niger Delta militants. Tompolo was charged to court in absentia in December 2016 with alleged money laundering offenses and declared "wanted by the government" when he failed to appear in court to answer to the charges. The ex-warlord has remained underground. Even though there have been all kinds of rumors, there have been no sighting of him. The police and the security forces have not been able to locate or arrest the ex-warlord or produce him in court even after an arrest warrant was issued by a Federal High Court in Abuja, the capital city, in January 2017.

This research inquiry investigated the underlying issues fueling the protracted conflicts associated with oil production in the Niger Delta region in Nigeria. Why have the conflicts lingered? What are the factors behind the resurgence of militant groups like the NDA several years after the introduction of the amnesty program? This inquiry investigated these questions. Table 1.1 below provides a brief comparison between activism during the era of Saro-Wiwa and contemporary insurgencies.

DEFINITION OF TERMS

It is pertinent in this section to define two key terms used in this study—perceptions and grievances.

Perceptions

The *Webster's Dictionary* defines perception as the ability to take hold of, feel or comprehend, to grasp mentally, to take note of, to become aware of through sight, hearing, touch, taste, or smell. Broadly, our perception of objects or situations depends on their context, the conditions in which they function (Kriesberg & Dayton, 2012). Lewicki, Barry, and Saunders (2010) posit that perception is the process by which individuals connect to their environment, while Steers (1984) defines perception as "the process of screening, selecting, interpreting stimuli so that they have meaning to the individual" (p. 98).

Many factors influence how a person understands and assigns meaning to messages and events. In this study, perception entails the expression of a point of view on a concerned issue by a person or a group of persons according to

Table 1.1 Activism in the Saro-Wiwa Era versus Era of Militancy

Saro-Wiwa and MOSOP 1990–1995	*MEND and Militancy 2005–present*
Charismatic leadership, visible, identifiable	Diffused leadership, underground, anonymous, use aliases or nicknames
Intellectually driven, idealistic, visionary	Passionate, frustrated, angry, bitter, feel left out
Utilized peaceful methods of mobilization, vigils, church services, and social media	Armed and utilized violent methods
Mixture of matured activists including chiefs, elders, and traditional rulers, youth, and women	Mostly made up of youths and teenagers, including female
Patriotic, projected community interests, not easily co-opted	Opportunistic, driven by personal economic interests; amenable to co-optation
Membership limited to the Ogoni people who inhabit five local governments in Rivers State	Most oil-producing communities in the Niger Delta are members or are sympathetic
Used the media, mass rallies, and protests to draw attention to their demands	Engages in kidnapping and ransoming of oil workers
Utilized local and international non-government organizations (NGOs) like Greenpeace, Amnesty International, and the United Nations for advocacy	Militants blow up oil infrastructure. In violent confrontation with the government and oil companies; operate artisan, private refineries and sells "stolen" crude oil locally and on the high seas
Key leaders, like Saro-Wiwa, jailed, put on trial, and executed	Key leaders awarded surveillance contracts by the government to protect oil shipping
Demobilized and weakened by heavy government crackdown	Uses violent attacks to attract the attention of the government and the oil companies
Thousands of activists driven into exile	Some elements work in cahoots with the security forces for pecuniary gains

Source: Generated by the author.

their understanding. Relating to resource governance and conflict in the Niger Delta the perceptions of the people are captured in interviews, NIIA media reports, databases, and government publications.

Grievances

Grievances are references to injustices perceived to be suffered by an individual or a group. It has been argued that

> the condition that receives most analytic and popular attention in explaining the emergence of a conflict is the grievance felt by at least one adversary, since contending groups usually account for their entering a conflict by referring to the injustices they suffer. (Kriesberg & Dayton, 2012, 59)

A sense of grievance, broadly speaking, often arises from within each possible adversary, from their relations with each other and from their social context. A grievance often combines consensual and dissensual elements, as Kriesberg and Dayton (2012) put it, "as happens when members of a minority community feel that they suffer discrimination for their views or way of life . . . they are denied access to goods and resources they believe they should have" (p. 60). As used in this study, grievances refer to simmering complaints by the people of the Niger Delta about perceived denials of access rights and unfair treatment by government and oil companies.

The conditions in the Niger Delta could be comparable, in some respects, to Colombia and to the economic crisis in Venezuela. Reuters reported that the leftist National Liberation Army (ELN) has allegedly carried out twelve attacks on Colombian pipelines in 2019 alone. The ELN opposes multinational companies, saying they seize natural resources without benefiting Colombians (Murphy, 2019). In 2017, Venezuela's oil revenue accounted for 98 percent of export revenue at 2.02 million barrels per day (OPEC, 2019), and yet had 27.1 percent unemployment while the country relies on imports to meet its basic food and consumer goods needs. The people face widespread shortages of goods, medicine, and medical supplies (CIA Factbook, 2019).

FIVE KEY SETS OF QUESTIONS HAVE GUIDED THIS STUDY

First, how does resource governance impact protracted resource conflicts in Nigeria's Niger Delta?

Second, what are the identities and agendas of actors and networks in the Niger Delta conflict?

Third, how does perception of relative deprivation of human needs contribute to the persistence of conflicts?

Fourth, what roles do Nigeria's political structures play in the emergence, sustenance, and resurgence of resource conflicts?

Finally, in what ways do mobilization methods of conflict actors affect the relationship between oil corporations and host communities?

AN ARGUMENT FOR THE RESOURCE GOVERNANCE TOOL

This study advances five main arguments. First, *Resource Governance and Protracted Conflicts in Nigeria's Niger Delta* argues that in the context of the Niger Delta, the resource governance school of thought presents the most convincing set of propositions to understanding and analyzing conflicts associated with natural resources in the Nigerian federation. Resource governance propositions capture the key elements that are critical to managing resource conflicts—the political systems, social relations, stakeholders and actors, elite networks, institutions, and regulations governing them. In this study, I combined resource governance school of thought briefly examined below with Edward Azar's protracted social conflict theory (PSC) to help better explain resource conflicts in the Nigerian federation. Political system, social relations, stakeholders, key actors, elite networks, institutions, and government regulations are critical to understanding and managing the Niger Delta conflicts.

Second, the character and environment of conflict, identities of actors, and the impact of the conflicts on the livelihood of the local communities have changed over the decades. The identities of the actors have changed; the style, strategy, the networks, and the methods of struggle have changed in response to alleged military crackdown by the government.

While the traditional actors and stakeholders such as the federal government, the IOCs, and host communities remain key players in the Niger Delta conflicts, the most changes have been noticed in the identities, agenda, and influences of the youth, community agitators, and informal networks of economic actors on the ground. The actors are younger, including youth from several other ethnic groups in the Niger Delta, beyond the Ogoni who started the struggle; they operate underground, feel more alienated and are hardened, and are now armed and adopt violent means as opposed to the peaceful agitation of the early days, and prone to risk co-optation.

Third, there are three layers of perception of deprivation among the citizens of the Niger Delta. First, is the perception that there is backwardness and lack of development in the region in comparison to other parts of Nigeria that do not produce crude oil. The feeling that the oil resources of the Niger Delta have been used and continue to be used to develop other cities and regions in Nigeria while they lack the basic social services like pipe-borne running water, electricity, healthcare facilities, and good schools. This stems from the awareness that the budgets of the three tiers of government—federal, state, and local governments—are mostly funded from the proceeds of crude oil and gas production.

Second, there is the perception that while the oil-producing communities in the Nigeria's Niger Delta lack the basic social services, the campsites or location sites of the oil companies exploiting crude oil and gas in the area have all the comfort of those social amenities. This is a source of discontent. The surrounding communities live in darkness, without electricity and clean pipeborn water and other basic services, while the living quarters and offices of the oil companies have social services comparable to what obtains in Lagos, and other cities in the United States or the western world. Third, there is the general perception of marginalization. The reason that the oil communities are neglected is that they are minorities and have no political leverage in the scheme of things in Nigeria. I must emphasize that these are long-held and deep-seated perceptions of the people.

My fourth argument is that the federal government controls the natural resources and those who own the land from which the oil and gas are produced are, broadly speaking, excluded from the benefits in a lopsided operation of a federation. This, my study shows, is done through the enactment of decrees and constitutional adjustments by several military regimes that take away the ownership rights of the Niger Delta communities to oil and gas resources exploited in their territory. This is a huge conflict trigger and consistently arises in discussions, petitions, and writings as the people believe that the political structure is skewed against them.

Finally, collected data suggests resource governance is both at the heart of the resource conflicts in the Niger Delta and the ideal place to find solutions. Anyone interested in understanding and proffering solutions to the Niger Delta conflicts would need to pay close attention to the complex nature of resource governance and its impact on conflict in the region. The dominant role and influence of transnational oil companies in Nigeria's economy, the impact of their activities on the livelihood and traditional occupations of the local people, the distortions, and dislocations, and the environment damage that the oil industry have caused require immediate reformation and mitigation to increase the prospect of de-escalation. My study identified what I would like to call *six cardinal pillars of resource governance,* namely, land rights, resource control, revenue sharing, community participation in the oil industry, provision of basic amenities, and environmental pollution and mitigation.

A BRIEF NOTE ON METHOD

In this study, I combined the resource governance school of thought with Edward Azar's PSC theory to better explain resource conflicts in the Nigerian federation. I utilized the Nigeria Institute of International Affairs (NIIA) research collection on the Niger Delta, databases such as Fund for Peace and Nigeria Watch, newspaper reports, expert opinions, government publications, and extensive semi-structured interviews at fieldwork sites in Bayelsa State and Rivers State.

Organization of Study

This study comprises seven chapters. In the present chapter, I introduced and provided a general overview of the study and discussed five sets of questions that guided the research and my main arguments. I also briefly discussed the method of inquiry and organization of the work.

Chapter 2 provides the detailed background and historical context of study as it is critical not only to understand the events, developments, and personalities that have shaped the history of the Niger Delta but also to highlight their context.

Chapter 3 provides an insightful discussion on the nexus between resource governance, the state, and protracted conflict. Why resource governance?

Chapter 4, "Six Cardinal Pillars of Resource governance," discusses the six pillars: land rights, resource control, revenue sharing, community participation in the oil industry, provision of basic amenities, and environmental pollution and mitigation. Any policy measures proposed to address the grievances of the Niger Delta should be targeted at these six pillars.

Chapter 5, "In the Eyes of the People," discusses the perceptions and grievances of the people of the Niger Delta.

In Chapter 6, The Heart of the Matter: The Ideal Place to Seek Solutions," I examine the content of resource governance and specific examples of why resource governance is the ideal place to seek solutions to the conflict in the region.

Chapter 7, "Lessons and Takeaways for Leaders and the Rest of Us" highlights in detail the description and themes that emerge from the data and participants' responses. I discuss their implications.

In the concluding chapter, I summarize the main arguments of this work and based on my findings, I make specific suggestions regarding the emerging youthful actors in the oil-bearing communities versus the dominant state actors and transnational oil companies. Next, I turn to discuss the background and historical context of the Niger Delta crises.

Chapter 2

Background and Historical Context of the Niger Delta Crises

COLONIAL NIGERIA

Nigeria is the most populous country in Africa. Located in the western coastline of the continent, Nigeria shares its borders with Benin in the west, Niger in the north, Chad in the northeast, and Cameroon to the east. The country began life as a loose collection of ethnic groups, nations, clans, and villages forcibly brought into being by British colonialism (Okonta & Douglas, 2001). Before the arrival of European explorers, missionaries, and colonialists, the territorial space known as Nigeria boast of empires such as Benin and Oyo, kingdoms such as Bonny and Opobo, and other heterogeneous societies in the southern regions as the Efik, Ogonis, Ibibios, and Ijaw of the Niger Delta.

Historical research indicates that the emergence of the geographical entity called Nigeria is attributable to three separate waves of British colonial activities. The southwestern part of Nigeria began with the conquest of Lagos in 1851 and the formal designation as crown colony in 1861 (Adebayo, 1993). On the Eastern front, British traders who operated trading posts around Niger Delta basin and adjacent creeks and rivers signed treaties with indigenous merchant chiefs, and the British used these treaties after the Berlin conference to establish the Oil Rivers protectorate.

In 1900, the British colonial government, which granted the Royal Niger Company (RNC) the license to conduct mercantile and commercial trade in palm oil in the Niger Valley south of Idah, revoked its charter and bought out the company, combined the area administered by the RNC with the Oil River protectorate to form the Protectorate of Southern Nigeria. This new administrative unit was divided into Eastern, Central, Cross River, and Western Divisions. The majority Igbo ethnic group and the minorities of the Niger

Delta, the Ibibio, Ijaw, Ogoja, and Ogoni peoples were included in the first three divisions (Okonta, 2008).

Nigeria formally became a federation in 1954. Scholars have proposed that there is strong evidence that the British imposed federalism on Nigeria as a continuation of its colonial experiments earlier tested in Canada, Australia, and South Africa. Adebayo (1993), for example, argues that,

> Whenever the British were faced with identical problems of governing large and ethnically diverse tropical dependencies, they quickly adopted this familiar scheme of federating peoples who probably would have existed as separate units, or who needed more cohesive integration. (pp. 20–21)[1]

Adebayo further proposes that the formal adoption of the federal system of government in 1954 was preceded by a transitional period of seven years during which various attributes of federalism were introduced by the Richards Constitution of 1946 and the Macpherson Constitution of 1951. Among the main features of Nigeria's federalism is the creation of three regions, North, West, and East, each of which exercised full legislative and executive authority within its area of jurisdiction. The constitutional provisions of 1954 created an Exclusive List on which only the federal government can legislate, a Concurrent List in which both the federal and regional governments could exercise jurisdiction, and a third Residual List that identified subject matters reserved for the regional governments.

Nigeria gained independence from Britain on October 1, 1960. The country was composed of three regions—Eastern Region with headquarters located in Enugu, Western Region whose headquarters was in Ibadan, and the Northern Region with headquarters in Kaduna.

THE WILLINK COMMISSION OF INQUIRY INTO THE FEARS OF MINORITIES

During the 1953 constitutional conference held in London to discuss a new constitution for Nigeria, and during subsequent talks leading up to Nigeria's impending independence, protagonists of the creation of states in Nigeria such as Harold Dappa-Biriye and Wenike Briggs, supported by official delegates of the National Convention of Nigerian Citizens (NCNC) from Ogoni like Timothy Paul Birabi, demanded protections and special treatment for the people of the Niger Delta. Their fear and argument were that the more populous ethnic groups in the emerging nation were likely to dominate and usurp the rights of the minority heterogeneous groups.

These protagonists needed assurances and security of fair treatment and even access to resources and development. Dappa-Biriye and other Niger

Delta politicians formed the Niger Delta Congress and joined with the Rivers State Association and the Ogoni State Representative Assembly both headed by Birabi, the NCNC member representing Ogoniland in the Eastern House of Assembly, in demanding the Niger Delta be considered a special area in the proposed new political arrangement. The rationale was the peculiar geographical terrain of the Niger Delta and the development needs that are believed to be different from those of other parts of the Eastern region (Nnoli, 1980; Post, 1963).

The congressional delegates of the Niger Delta formally presented a demand for a new Rivers State to be carved out of the Eastern Region at the 1953 constitutional conference in London. Birabi participated as an NCNC delegate at the conference (Post, 1963). A second group of leaders and agitators from Eastern Nigeria who were opposed to the consolidation of the proposed three regions in Nigeria staged a walk-out at the 1953 London Constitutional talks and formed the Calabar, Ogoja, and Rivers State Movement (COR State Movement), and started to press for the creation of a separate state made up of Calabar, Ogoja, and Rivers provinces.

Preparatory to the 1957 Constitutional Conference, the Rivers Chiefs and Peoples Conference was formed in July 1956 to replace the Council of Rivers chiefs and it fully supported the Rivers State Movement which the COR leaders were naturally opposed to (Okonta, 2008). All five Ogoni clans were fully represented in the Rivers Chiefs and Peoples Conference. Indeed, the demand for Rivers State gathered momentum after the London Constitutional talks. When the constitutional talks resumed in 1957, the leaders of the Rivers Chiefs and Peoples Conference had two key arguments:

- That the people in this area shared a way of life dictated by the physical circumstances of the country in which they lived, and that they were united by fear of might at the hands of a government who did not understand their needs, and who in any case put the needs of the interior first.
- That when the British first came to this area, they made treaties of trade and protection with loyal chiefs; these were of a special nature and differed from the treaties made with other chiefs inland. The British Crown undertook to provide protection and to deal with foreign powers, but the treaties did not provide that the chiefs should surrender to the British government a sovereignty, which could be transferred to any other authority. If Her Majesty's Government saw fit to end the treaties, then the chiefs of this area were morally entitled to revert to their original States (Saro-Wiwa, 1989, 89). This last point is critical and apropos to having a deeper insight into the underlying issues in the conflicts in the Niger Delta region.

The London Constitutional Conference of 1957 granted the Eastern and Western regions their request to be self-governing in addition to creating the office of a prime minister in Nigeria. These concessions heightened the fears of the political leaders in the minority areas that the majority groups would use their control of government to further dominate and marginalize them politically and economically. They requested that the creation of new states and regions for their people should be considered by the colonial government before granting independence to the country.

Rather than create states for the minority groups, the colonial government appointed the "Henry Willink Commission of Inquiry into the Fears of Minority Groups and the Means to Allaying Them." Sir Henry Willink, Master of Trinity College, Cambridge was made the head of the panel of inquiry. When the Willink Commission began sitting at Enugu in January 1958, the representatives of the COR State Movement, the Action Group Opposition in the Eastern Region House of Assembly, the Ogoja State Movement, and the representatives of the Asa, Diobu, Ikwerre, Ndoki, and Ogoni peoples were present. (Reports of the Commission as cited in Okonta, 2008, 73.)

The submissions and representations of the Ogoni people and other ethnic groups in the Niger Delta to the Willink Commission in 1958 and response of the dominant Igbo ethnic group that controlled the Eastern regional government at the time bears detailing, and I consider these events as the beginning of the Niger Delta political agitations to which economic and environmental agitations were added after petroleum production began. In his presentation in the commission, Suanu Finimale Nwika, NCNC member of the Federal House of Representatives for Ogoni Division, said that all five Ogoni clans were represented in the Rivers Chiefs and Peoples Conference, and that they fully supported the River State Movement because his people felt that they had been neglected by the regional government in Enugu. Specifically, he told the commission that:

- There was an inequitable distribution of amenities in the region. There were only 48 miles of road, and of 1,000 regional scholarships awarded from 1952 to 1956, only seven had been awarded to Ogoni.
- There were no industries. Of the 187 Pioneer Oil Mills[2] in the region not one was located in Ogoni Division.
- Postal and telegraph services were inadequate. There was no telegraph office in the Division and there were postal agencies in only two of the five clans.
- The Division was inadequately represented in the House of Representatives and in the House of Assembly.
- No Ogoni had ever been appointed a minister.
- They were completely unrepresented on Public Boards.

The Willink Commission failed to recommend the creation of states for minorities as demanded. In the particular case of the proposed Rivers State, the commission explained that the proposed Rivers State was not viable. Although the commission observed that there was widespread support for the new state in Brass, Degema, and Ogoni divisions, the last was divided from Brass and Degema by an arm of the sea and, also, by a long stretch of Igbo territory, making the prospects of such a state unfeasible. The commission decided not to create Rivers State in order not to create a new problem as the idea was resented by the Ibos.

The commission, however, recommended among other things, the creation of the Niger Delta Basin Development Board (NDBDB) to address the development needs and terrain of the Niger Delta region "because of the problems of development in this area of creeks and mangrove swamps" (Post, 1963, 4–5). While the generality of the people welcomed the idea of a development board, some of the leaders thought that the board was still-born given that all it could do was conduct research and make recommendations to various governments (Saro-Wiwa, 1989).

THE NIGER DELTA AND NIGERIA'S ECONOMY

The Niger Delta region refers to the geographical territory in southern Nigeria which covers some 43,500 square miles and is the largest river delta in Africa and the third largest in the world (United Nations Environment Program Report, 2011). This floodplain is home to about 10 million people, composed of several minority ethnic groups such as the Andoni, Edo, Efik, Etche, Ibibio, Ijaw, Isoko, Itshekiri, Ikwerre, Ogba, Ogoni, and Urhobo. Some of these ethnic groups are further divided into clans and sub-clans with their own distinctive languages (Dike, 1956).

The region has been of significant economic importance from precolonial times. Before the arrival of the European explorers and missionaries, the people of the Niger Delta traded with the people of the hinterland, particularly the Igbos. They exported dried fish, crayfish, and salt in exchange for fruit and iron tools. Slave trading was introduced by the Portuguese explorers in 1864 in the Niger Delta. The Atlantic slave trade was responsible for thousands of able-bodied young men and women taken from the region and its hinterland and shipped to plantations in North America, South America, and the West Indies. The slave trade brought with it great and social dislocations in the Niger Delta (Okonta & Douglas, 2001).

Before crude oil, there was palm oil. Following the abolition of slavery in the early 19th century there was a switch to the so-called "legitimate" trade in palm oil. The palm oil trade expanded as the pace of industrialization accelerated in Europe. Greater quantities of palm oil were required to lubricate machine parts and to produce margarine and soap for the thousands of factory workers who migrated to the cities. Indeed by 1856, Bonny had become the richest port in the Niger Delta, and the port and its hinterland were exporting over 25,000 tons of palm oil a year, over half of the total quantity exported for Africa (Dike, 1956).

Palm oil trade became more lucrative as the pace of industrialization increased in Europe and more quantities of pam oil were needed to lubricate machine parts and to produce soap and margarine for thousands of factory workers who migrated to the cities.

Indeed by 1856, Bonny had grown to be the richest port in the Niger Delta and its hinterland and was exporting over 25,000 tons of palm oil a year, over half of the total quantity exported from Africa (Dike, 1956). George Taubman arrived in the Niger Delta during the scramble for Africa and conducted a merger of several British firms to secure a monopoly over the palm oil trade. Obtaining a royal charter, he called his business the Royal Niger Company (RNC). He signed spate of treaties with coastal chiefs literally at gunpoint. Some scholars have suggested that it was Taubman who first integrated the Niger Delta economy into international economy:

> There is no doubt the George Goldie Taubman and the Royal Niger Company which he founded played a key role in bringing together the otherwise disparate nations and ethnic groups in the Niger Basin into what is now known as Nigeria. (Okonta & Douglas, 2001, 13)

Dike (1956) made a similar argument:

> Indeed, it can be said that the basis of the underdevelopment of the Niger Delta, following the forcible integration of the area into the world of international capital in the nineteenth century, was laid by Goldie Taubman and the Royal Niger Company in the 1890s. (Dike, 1956, 210)

Crude oil was first discovered in commercial quantities in Oloibiri in the Niger Delta in 1956 by Shell D'Arcy Oil. Nigerian authorities define commercial production as the output of over 10,000 barrels of crude oil a day. Shell's successful discovery of substantial oil deposits in Ebubu and Bomu in Ogoni area in 1958–1959 established Nigeria firmly as a major world provider of crude oil, making her the largest oil producer in Africa and the eighth largest oil producer in the world. Over the years Nigeria was to become a member of OPEC in 1971, producing 2.2 million barrels a day in 1993 compared to Saudi Arabia's 9.7 million barrels a day output (OPEC, 2018).

When civil war broke out in 1967, the Shell-BP venture was producing 580,000 barrels of oil per day from nine oil fields, generating 76 million pounds in yearly revenue to the Nigerian government from rents, royalties, premiums, profit taxes (Okonta, 2008). There were several American oil companies also active in the country during this period, but Shell-BP dominated the industry, accounting for three-fourths of total production (Wolpe, 1974). The fate of the Niger Delta people appears to have been altered for all time with the enactment of Decrees 51 of 1969 and Decree 6 of 1975 by the military government. When Shell D'Arcy (Shell Oil's operating name at the time) began oil exploration in colonial Nigeria, it did so under a 1937 Colonial Mineral Ordinance, an exclusive exploration and prospecting rights given it by the British Colonial Office. In 1938, the British government granted an Oil Exploration License that covered the entire country to Shell.

Nigeria's 1960 Independence Constitution had specified that revenue sharing be based on the principle of derivation. The regions were required under section 134 (1) of the 1960 Constitution, to give 50 percent of royalties and mining rents to the federal government and retain 50 percent. The Republican Constitution of 1963 also retained these provisions under Section (140) (1). Nigeria's military head of state, Lt. Col. Yakubu Gowon's decree 51 both annulled the 1937 ordinance and overturned the revenue allocation formula, following the dissolution of the regions by the decree in 1967 when states were created. It transferred ownership of mineral rights to the federal government (Khan, 1994). Decree 6 of 1975 increased the federal government's share of oil proceeds from 50 percent to 80 percent, leaving states with 20 percent. The foregoing is critically important as we shall see in chapter 5 as respondents during fieldwork interviews repeatedly allude to this aspect of resource governance.

The key feature of Nigeria's economy since the end of the civil war in 1970 has been crude oil production, mining, and marketing. The crude oil deposits are exploited in the bowels of the Niger Delta. Despite the region's abundant natural resources and its strategic importance to Nigerian economy and the world energy security, the area is marked by poverty, high unemployment, inequality, economic underdevelopment, and environmental pollution (UNDP, 2006). It has been estimated that between 1958, when commercial oil production commenced, and 1983, Nigeria earned \$101 billion (Dudley, 1982). Local communities, however, claim that oil production by transnational oil companies has brought with it huge impacts on them through the loss of agricultural cultivation, pollution of rivers and creeks, oil spills, and gas flaring.

CREATION OF STATES

As civil war loomed, Gowon proclaimed a decree and divided the country into twelve states out of the existing four regions on May 27, 1967. He appointed a military governor for each of the new states, proclaimed a State of Emergency throughout the country, imposed economic sanctions against Eastern Nigeria, and banned all political statements and meetings. The move was seen as a tactical, political calculation to persuade the minorities of Eastern Nigeria to deny their support for Lt. Col. Chukwemeka Odumegwu-Ojukwu, the military governor of the region, who had demanded a loose federation and more autonomy for his region. This was the aftermath of the assassination of former head of state, Lt. General Aguiyi Ironsi and the killings of Ibos and other citizens of the Eastern region resident in Northern Nigeria. The move was to lure the Eastern minorities to embrace the federal military government. In the next few paragraphs, I analyze the events that promoted the creation of the very states that the colonial administration refused.

Nigeria had been thrown into a new political path in January 1966 when young officers in the Nigerian army led by Major Chukwuma "Kaduna" Nzeogwu staged a military coup and attempted to take over the reins of power. The coup was a partial success. While the coup leaders could not take over the government, the civilian governments both at the federal and state levels were sacked and replaced by the military. The army chief, Major General J. T. U. Aguiyi Ironsi assumed the role of head of state and commander-in-chief of the armed forces. The country's first prime minister, Abubakar Tafawa Balewa, the premier of Northern region, Sir Ahmadu Bello, and the premier of Western region, Samuel L. Akintola were killed. Other senior military officers from the north such as Brigadier Maimalari, and Colonels Victor Pam and Largema were also assassinated in the putsch.

The key coup plotters, all with the rank of major, Chukwuma Nzeogwu, Emmanuel Ifeajuna, Adewale Ademoyega, and Ben Gbulie, were all from southern Nigeria. Given that no ranking Ibo politician was killed, a trending narrative emerged that the coup was anti-North and that the intent was for the Ibo to dislodge the Hausa-Fulani, the majority ethnic group in Northern Nigeria from power. Ironsi arrested the coup plotters and imprisoned them, suspended the Nigerian constitution and appointed Lt. Col. Adekunle Fajuyi as military governor of the Western region, Major Hassan Usman Katsina as military governor of the Northern region, Lt. Col. David Ejoor as military governor of the Mid-Western region, and Lt. Col. Chukwuemeka Odumegwu-Ojukwu as military governor of Eastern Nigeria (Saro-Wiwa, 1989).

The Ironsi government initiated a few corruption probes and set up a committee to examine the question of writing a new constitution. Then in February 1966, a surprising secession attempt appeared in the Niger Delta area, a sign of coming political unrest in the area. Isaac Adaka Boro, a former police officer and a student at the University of Nigeria, Nsukka, from the Ijaw ethnic group in the Niger Delta, led a group of young militia men and overran several police posts in the Rivers Province. Boro, declared a "Niger Delta Republic." In his posthumously published book, *The Twelve Day-Revolution*, Boro (1982) says,

> A Niger Delta State is a clear case as the people concerned have a distinct historical silhouette. Such a demand becomes all the more compelling when the area is so viable, yet the people are blatantly denied development and the common necessities of life. If Nigerian government refuse to do something to drastically improve the lot of the people, inevitably, a point of no return will be reached; then evil is afoot. (p. 16)

The aim of his "revolution," he asserts, was

> to present an action front and dissociate entirely the Niger Delta area from any support whatsoever of the newly-formed military government of Nigeria. In this respect, therefore, we were to break the Niger Delta Area away into a nation and strive to maintain it. (Boro, 1982, 16)

The military government swiftly moved in against Boro and captured him. The Eastern Nigeria High Court tried and sentenced him to death for treason.

In May 1966, riots broke out in the Northern region. Ibos and southerners were targets of riots, violence, arson, and looting (Okonta, 2008). In July 1966, a counter coup led by officers from "the North," was launched and Major General Ironsi was assassinated during a visit to Ibadan in the Western region, along with his host, Lt. Col. Adekunle Fajuyi, the military governor of the region. There were more killings and persecution of southerners in the North. Lt. Col. Yakubu Gowon emerged as head of state. In a broadcast to the nation, Gowon stated that there was no basis to the unitary system that General Ironsi had sought to impose on the people and revoked the decree promulgated by Ironsi.

To douse tension, Gowon instituted an Ad-hoc Committee on Constitutional Issues to discuss among other matters, the issue of states creation. And then in April 1967, the Supreme Military Council, the highest organ of the military government, announced that a States Creation Committee would be set up to recommend on the number and identity of states that need to be created in Nigeria. In an address to diplomats in Lagos at the end of April, Lt. Col. Gowon stated that he would create the COR state as a means of protecting minorities in Eastern Nigeria if Lt. Col. Ojukwu persisted with his secessionist plan.

In a swift reaction, Dappa-Biriye, a key leader of the Rivers State Movement, released a public statement to the press:

> With due deference to the Federal Military Government, I wish to register this protest with you on behalf of Rivers people in an open letter against your declared intention to create a COR STATE, possibly by force, as a means of retaining minorities of Eastern Nigeria origin in the Federation, if Lt. Col. Odumegwu Ojukwu decided to secede. Over 95% of Rivers people abhor the idea of a COR STATE. This is not because Rivers people dislike the other Eastern minorities but because a COR STATE is unrealistic and administratively impossible. We want a Rivers State pure and simple owing to the fundamental difference in the environment of the Rivers area from those of all its neighboring groups in Nigeria; and we are sure that a Rivers State will be able to pay its way as a direct unit of the Nigerian federation and will protect itself in peace and war like any other unit. (Saro-Wiwa, 1989, 144)

Thus, Rivers State with capital in Port Harcourt was created along with eleven other states on May 27, 1967.

NIGERIAN CIVIL WAR

States creation did not prevent the drift to war. The Nigerian civil war broke out on July 6, 1967, when Nigerian federal forces fired shots at Biafran locations in the southeastern border of the Nigeria with the new Biafran republic at a border village called Gakem in Cross River State. Gowon announced to the country that he had ordered "police action" against Biafra. Lt. Col. Ojukwu had proclaimed the Republic of Biafra on May 30, 1967, breaking away the Eastern Region of Nigeria to form a new country, barely three days after Gowon divided Nigeria into twelve states.

There are few points that are important concerning the conduct of the Nigerian Civil War that are relevant for this study.

- The release of political prisoners. Key political prisoners including the officers who carried out the coup of January 1966 were set free. Isaac Boro, for example, was released and co-opted to lead the war effort to capture Port Harcourt from the Biafran forces.
- Most Eastern minorities appear to have supported the war efforts on the federal side.
- Total number of deaths is estimated at about 2 million. The Ogoni people in the Niger Delta estimated that they lost about 30,000 souls during the war.

- Economic blockade ordered by the federal government against Biafra caused economic hardship, stress, and pain for the general population. The cost of living was high and household essentials were scarce and when found prices were expensive and out of reach for most people. The cost of salt, for example, was four times its normal price.

The war lasted until January 1970 when the Biafran Commander Phillip Effiong surrendered to federal forces and signed the pact to end the war with Col. Olusegun Obasanjo of the federal side (Akpan, 1971). Observers of Nigerian politics draw the conclusion that the long-lasting outcome of the Nigerian civil war was the introduction and acceptance of military ethos into governance and social relations. The military rules by decree, by martial law. The country is a federation, but it was being run as a unitary state given the hierarchical nature of the military organization. Ike Okonta and Oronto Douglas (2001), for example, argue that

> The civil war was a watershed in the political and economic development of the peoples of the Niger Delta, creating the conditions for accelerated exploitation of their resources and the devastation of their environment. (p. 23)

THE OGONI BILL OF RIGHTS AND MOSOP

In 1990, the Ogoni people, a minority ethnic group in the Niger Delta began a nonviolent resistance campaign against the Nigerian government and the transnational oil companies operating in their indigenous territory. The struggle was the brainchild of a famous writer, Ken Saro-Wiwa. Under the auspices of MOSOP he hosted a series of meetings with chiefs, traditional rulers, the clergy, teachers, community leaders, opinion leaders, the intelligentsia, and political leaders in January 1990.

Saro-Wiwa convinced his fellow Ogonis on the need to organize to change their social condition (Saro-Wiwa, 1995). He presented a draft copy of the Ogoni Bill of Rights (OBR) which he singlehandedly wrote for review and debate. The draft copies of the bill were taken to districts and villages in all six kingdoms of Ogoni for input and comments. In August 1990, the chiefs, elders, and leaders of Ogoni signed the OBR, and it was ratified by popular acclaim by the generality of the people present (Dibua, 2004).

The OBR laid out in its sixteen pages the underlying circumstances, historical, and social background to the struggle. The key demand is political autonomy or self-determination by whatever name called, comprising the four cardinal points of the struggle:

- Political control of Ogoni affairs by Ogoni people;
- The right to the control and use of a fair proportion of Ogoni economic resources for Ogoni development;
- Adequate and direct representation as of right in all Nigerian national institutions; and
- The right to protect the Ogoni environment and ecology from further degradation. (MOSOP, 1990)

The Ogoni Bill of Rights put forward a strong argument for the development of Ogoni territory with the enormous resources in natural gas and crude oil exploited by transnational oil companies and it argued are used to develop other parts of Nigeria. It also called for measures to mitigate the environmental impact of oil production on the community and demanded compensation for loss of land and rents since oil exploitation began in their territory. Indeed, the OBR explicitly states that the goal of self-determination of the Ogoni people is within the ambit of the Nigerian federation.[3]

The OBR was presented to the government and people of Nigeria in October 1990 but "an appeal to the international community" was added in December 1991. A few months after the signing of the OBR by the chiefs and elders of Ogoni, MOSOP was inaugurated as the vehicle for implementing the nonviolent campaign to achieve the objectives set out in the OBR.

MOSOP is an umbrella body, the most important sociocultural organization of the Ogoni people. It comprises several affiliate grassroots organizations such as the National Youth Council of the Ogoni People, Council of Ogoni Professionals, Federation of Ogoni Women Associations, Ogoni Teachers Union, National Union of Ogoni Students, Ogoni Central Union, and Council of Ogoni Traditional Rulers.

Leaders elected from these bodies constitute the decision-making organ of MOSOP known as the Steering Committee and they met monthly. The mobilization of MOSOP members started with the staging of rallies at Kingdom and district headquarters and weekly and monthly meetings within the various affiliate organizations. Speakers at the rallies and meetings would discuss the various aspects of the resistance and explain the reasons why the struggle was being embarked upon and how important it was for everyone to participate.

The event that made the Ogoni struggle nationally and internationally known was the public protest of January 4, 1993. Tagged "Ogoni Day in the United Nations Year of the World's Indigenous Peoples 1993," the event witnessed 300,000 Ogonis, who took to the streets with leaves, placards, and signs to denounce Shell Oil and the policies of the government of Nigeria. The participants utilized songs, cultural dances, street theaters, masquerades, and colorful banners to protest in a festive and carnival style. They called for an end to gas flaring and environmental pollution in Ogoni. The participants cut across every section of the Ogoni society, the young and old, male, and female, the educated and uneducated, rich, and poor, the employed and the unemployed, students, traders, fishermen, and farmers.

Greenpeace and Rainforest Action Network sent observers to the protest. The independent press in Nigeria also covered the march. *Newswatch*, the most influential private newsmagazine in the country at the time, did a full cover story on the protest march (Waidor-Prebagha, 1993). The story also attracted a great deal of international attention with wide coverage in *New York Times*, *CNN*, and *The Guardian* of London.

THE EXECUTION OF KEN SARO-WIWA AND EIGHT OTHER OGONI ACTIVISTS

A tragedy occurred on May 21, 1994, when four prominent Ogoni chiefs and elders were murdered in questionable circumstances in Gionkoo, the traditional headquarters of the Gokana kingdom of Ogoni during an alleged rioting at a gathering unconnected with MOSOP. Saro-Wiwa was arrested and the military administrator of Rivers State, Lt. Col. Dauda Komo, accused MOSOP members of being responsible for the deaths of the chiefs and elders in a press conference. The military administrator declared that several key officials of MOSOP were wanted in connection with the murders and ordered 3,000 soldiers into Ogoni (Senewo, 2015). All roads leading out of Ogoni were cordoned off and all vehicles were stopped and searched. On the pretext of searching for the suspects who murdered the four elders, massive human rights violations were alleged to have been perpetrated by the soldiers.

Saro-Wiwa and hundreds of Ogoni men and women were detained in several detention centers—including the Bori Camp Military Base, the Military Detention Facility in Afam, the State Criminal Investigation Department Detention Center in Port Harcourt, and the Kpor Detention Facility established by the Task Force—for several months. In November 1994, Nigeria's military ruler, General Abacha, convened a Civil Disturbances Special Tribunal, consisting of two judges and a serving military officer to try cases arising from the Gionkoo disturbances. On January 28, 1995, a group of five defendants, namely, Saro-Wiwa, Ledum Mitee, Barinem Kiobel, John Kpuinen, and Baribor Bera, were charged. Of these, the first three accused were said to have encouraged the killing of the four murder victims, while Bera and Kpuinen were alleged to be among the actual killers. On February 28, 1995, two additional groups of five were charged; all ten accused were alleged to have participated in the killings (Birnbaum, 1995).

Independent observers, including Nigerian and foreign legal experts and the United Nations, described the proceedings of the Tribunal as a travesty of justice (Birnbaum, 1995; United Nations, 1996). On October 31, 1995, the Tribunal sentenced Saro-Wiwa and eight of the ten accused to death by hanging. Saro-Wiwa and eight of his fellow detainees were hanged in Port Harcourt prisons on November 10, 1995 (Birnbaum, 1995).[4] The United Nations, the British Commonwealth, and world leaders, including Nelson Mandela, condemned the executions. British Prime Minister John Major described the executions as "judicial murder."

THE KAIAMA DECLARATION

Saro-Wiwa's mobilization of the Ogoni people spurned similar efforts by other minority ethnic groups in the Niger Delta. In October 1992, the Ijaw people established the Movement for the Survival of the Izon Ethnic Nationality and presented the Izon Peoples Charter to the country. Modeled loosely on the OBR, the Charter called for political autonomy for Ijaw people in a restructured Nigerian federation and adequate compensation for ecological adversities suffered during years of oil production in their land (Okonta & Douglas, 2001). In 1993, the Council of Ikwerre Nationality was established to articulate the demands of the community based on justice and fairness. In response to the hanging of Saro-Wiwa and co-travelers, other Niger Delta groups began to explore violent means of advocacy other than the peaceful agitation.

On December 11, 1998, over 5,000 youths drawn from 500 communities and 40 clans of Ijaw group converged in the village of Kaiama and established the Ijaw Youth Council (IYC) and issued the Kaiama Declaration. Cataloging the "unabating damage done to fragile natural environment and to the health of our people due to the exploration of crude oil" the IYC demanded that "all oil companies stop all exploration and exploitation activities in the Ijaw area" (Okonta & Douglas, 2001, 145). One of the militant groups to emerge on the scene to carry on the agitation of the people of the region during the period of my study is the Niger Delta Avengers (NDA). CNBC, an American news network reported in 2016 the Avengers are driven by economic and environmental grievances and were in the business of destroying oil infrastructure—working in teams, carrying small arms and explosives, and blowing up pipelines and sabotaging facilities.

The foregoing constitutes a detailed review of the relevant background and historical context of my study. It was important to engage in this review to establish the background to the protracted nature of the Niger Delta conflict and that the fears of marginalization by the Niger Delta ethnic groups started during colonial times, continued during the civil war, and appeared to have been proven right with the execution of Saro-Wiwa and his fellow activists. To summarize, the conflict began as peaceful protests among the leadership elite under colonial rule and in the immediate aftermath of independence. Political issues were dominant and sharing of governmental offices and resources was at the forefront, but the overall concern seemed to be the marginalization of the region. At the time petroleum resources were not yet the focus. This changed after the civil war. Even then, the immediate response was peaceful protest by the minority groups of the Niger Delta. The conflict turned violent after the execution of Ken Saro-Wiwa in 1995. In the next chapter, I discuss the nexus between resource governance, the state, and protracted conflict.

NOTES

1. See Adebayo (1993, 14–27) for exhaustive discussion on this section.
2. A Pioneer Oil Mill was a simple processing facility of intermediate scale, in which the material is still handled manually between the processing stages, designed by the Africa United Company to process about three-quarters of a ton of palm fruit per hour, which is the equivalent of about one ton of fruit bunches, following the removal of the fruit from the bunch stalks.
3. The Ogoni Bill of Rights clearly states: "Now, therefore, while reaffirming our wish to remain a part of the Federal Republic of Nigeria, we make demand on the Republic as follows" (MOSOP, 1991, 11).
4. In Nigeria, this is commonly referred to as "The hanging of the OGONI 9."

Chapter 3

Understanding the Nexus between Resource Governance, the State, and Protracted Conflict

WHAT IS RESOURCE GOVERNANCE?

Governance refers to the institutional capability of public organizations to provide the public and other goods demanded by a country's citizens or their representatives in an effective, transparent, impartial, and accountable manner. The Mo Ibrahim Foundation (2018) defines governance as "the provision of the political, social, and economic public goods and services that every citizen has the right to expect from their state, and that a state has the responsibility to deliver to its citizens." The foundation developed the Ibrahim Index of African Governance (IIAG), which identifies four key components of measuring performance in delivering governance in African countries. The four categories include safety and rule of law, participation and human rights, sustainable economic opportunity, and human development (Ibrahim, 2018). The IIAG is a tool that annually measures and monitors governance performance in fifty-four African countries. Nigeria was ranked thirty-three in 2018. Established in 2007, the index is considered the most robust and up-to-date dashboard on the state of governments in every African country.

Resource governance, a subset of governance as utilized in this study, entails the institutional mechanisms and political will embedded in the management of natural resources. "These mechanisms involve considerations such as domestic laws, constitutional provisions, cultural practices, customary laws, neo-patrimonial practices, and all the international treaties and obligations that govern issues such as the ownership, management, extraction, revenue sharing, enforcement capacity, and the procedures for addressing concerns and grievances over natural resources" (Alao, 2007, 31). In this study, natural resources in the broadest sense, is referencing crude oil and gas resources exploited and produced in Nigeria's Niger Delta, the mainstay of the Nigerian economy. Resource governance essentially refers to all the internal and external considerations that come to play in the management of natural resources. Some of these considerations include constitutional provisions, customary laws, international treaties, and obligations regulating ownership, extraction, management, and sharing of natural resources within a given country (Alao, 2007). Scholars such as Watts (2015) and Williams (2011) argue that resource governance should include the examination of the murky alliances between local political, military, and business elites and transnational firms and the desire of wielders of power to maintain control of the institutions of state power. It was critical to discuss the concept of resource governance given its centrality to my study—the impact of resource governance on enduring resource conflicts in Nigeria's Niger Delta. The concept is a constant refrain throughout the study from the data collection all the way to the analysis phase.

Protracted conflicts as used in this study refer to intractable conflicts that appear to be difficult to resolve. Coleman (2006) says, "intractable conflicts are essentially conflicts that persist because they appear impossible to resolve" (p. 534). Several scholars have studied and used labels such as *deeply rooted conflict* (Burton, 1987), *protracted social conflict* (Azar, 1990), *enduring rivalries* (Goertz & Diehl, 1993), and *moral conflict* (Pearce & Littlejohn, 1997) to describe similar phenomena. Conflict is an outgrowth of the diversity that characterizes thoughts, attitudes, beliefs, perceptions, social systems, and structures. Conflicts associated with natural resources (crude oil) in Nigeria manifest both violently and nonviolently and involve state and non-state actors. In this investigation, I define conflict as the manifestation of incompatible goals, objectives, and interests of parties involved in a struggle for power or resources.

My inquiry focuses on conflicts that are associated with revenue derived from the production and sale of natural resources, specifically oil and gas in Nigeria. It is important to discuss the nature of conflicts in the Niger Delta as a background to answering my central research question: how does resource governance impact protracted conflicts in Nigeria's Niger Delta? In Nigeria states are political and administrative division of centers of power in a federation, the second tier of government. There are thirty-six states in the Nigerian federation. Each state is administered by an executive governor, has an elected House of Assembly, the legislative arm of government, and a judiciary, made up of high courts, magistrate courts, and customary courts. Aspects of Azar's theory utilized in the study are linked to multiculturalism and pluralism as briefly discussed above and the role of states and ethnic groups in the Niger Delta conflicts are crucial to understanding the onset, escalation, persistence, and resurgence of conflicts. States are composed of ethnic group, communities and villages including oil-bearing communities that are of significant interest in this study.

Oil-producing communities are the towns and villages on whose land, creeks, and rivers are found huge deposits of crude oil and natural gas. These communities are hosts to oil fields, flow stations, oil wells, flow lines, manifolds (junctions of pipes), tank farms, pipelines, loading and shipping decks, export terminals, gas fares, depots, and gas filling stations operated by transnational oil corporations like Shell, Chevron, Eni-Agip, Elf, Texaco, Mobil, Total, Statoil/BP, Phillips, Amoco, and Conoco. Besides the burden of losing agricultural land to oil installations, members of these communities also contend with the impact of oil operations on their daily lives including environmental damage and pollution. It is important to discuss and understand who the host communities are as they represent the communal content in the theory and conceptual framework. It is equally important to highlight the substance of the Niger Delta, in terms of the communities and the territory.

Nigeria's Niger Delta refers to the nine states in the south of Nigeria that contain the oil and gas deposits that provide the bulk of federal revenue. These states are Abia, Akwa Ibom, Bayelsa, Cross River, Delta, Edo, Imo Ondo, and Rivers. According to the 2006 census, the Niger Delta constitutes 23 percent of Nigeria's population with over 30 million inhabitants with an estimated population density of 265 persons per square mile. The Niger Delta comprises 185 out of 774 local government areas (LGAs) in Nigeria.

In this research, Niger Delta region refers to the geographical territory in southern Nigeria which covers some 43,500 square miles and is the largest river delta in Africa and the third largest in the world (United Nations Environment Program Report, 2011). Despite the region's abundant natural resources and its importance to Nigerian economy, the area is marked by poverty, high unemployment, inequality, economic underdevelopment, and environmental pollution (UNEP, 2011).

RESEARCH QUESTIONS

As discussed in chapter 1 the purpose of this study was to explore and better understand how resource governance impacts protracted conflicts in the Niger Delta, Nigeria. My main research question was, how does resource governance impact protracted conflicts in Nigeria's Niger Delta? The subsidiary questions were:

- What are the identities and agendas of stakeholders and networks in the Niger Delta conflicts?
- How does the perception of relative deprivation of human needs contribute to the persistence of the conflicts?

- What roles do Nigeria's political structures play in the emergence, sustenance, and resurgence of resource conflicts?
- In what ways do mobilization methods of conflict actors affect the relationship between transnational oil corporations and oil-producing communities?

OPERATIONALIZATION OF KEY CONCEPTS

As shown in figure 3.1, I operationalized Azar's theory of protracted social conflicts to answer my central research question. I asked subsidiary questions to provide answer to my main research question. To expatiate the communal content of PSC, I inquired, what are the identities, agendas, and networks of actors in the Niger Delta? Probing deprivation of human needs as the underlying source of conflict, I inquired, how does perception of relative human needs contribute to the persistence of conflicts? And to examine the nature of the state, I posed the question, what roles do political structures play in the emergence, sustenance, and resurgence of resource conflicts? Finally, to explicate international linkages, I inquired, in what ways do mobilization methods of conflict actors affect relationships between oil corporations and host communities? My main research question and subsidiary questions are borne out of my literature review and conceptual framework.

This conceptual framework (figure 3.2) depicts an attempt to understand resource governance and its impact on conflicts related to oil production and distribution within the Nigerian federation. Starting with the top mid-section, resource governance entails constitutional provisions and political

Operationalization of Azar's PSC

Main Research Question	Main question: How does resource governance impact protracted resource conflicts in Nigeria's Niger Delta?
a. communal content of PSC	a. What are the identities & agendas of actors & networks in the Niger Delta conflict?
b. deprivation of human needs as the underlying source of conflict	b. How does perception of relative deprivation of human needs contribute to the persistence of the conflicts?
c. nature of the state	c. What roles do Nigeria's political structures play in the emergence, sustenance, & resurgence of resource conflicts?
d. international linkages	d. In what ways do mobilization methods of conflict actors affect the relationship between oil corporations & host communities?

Figure 3.1 Operationalization of Azar's PSC. *Source*: Generated by the author.

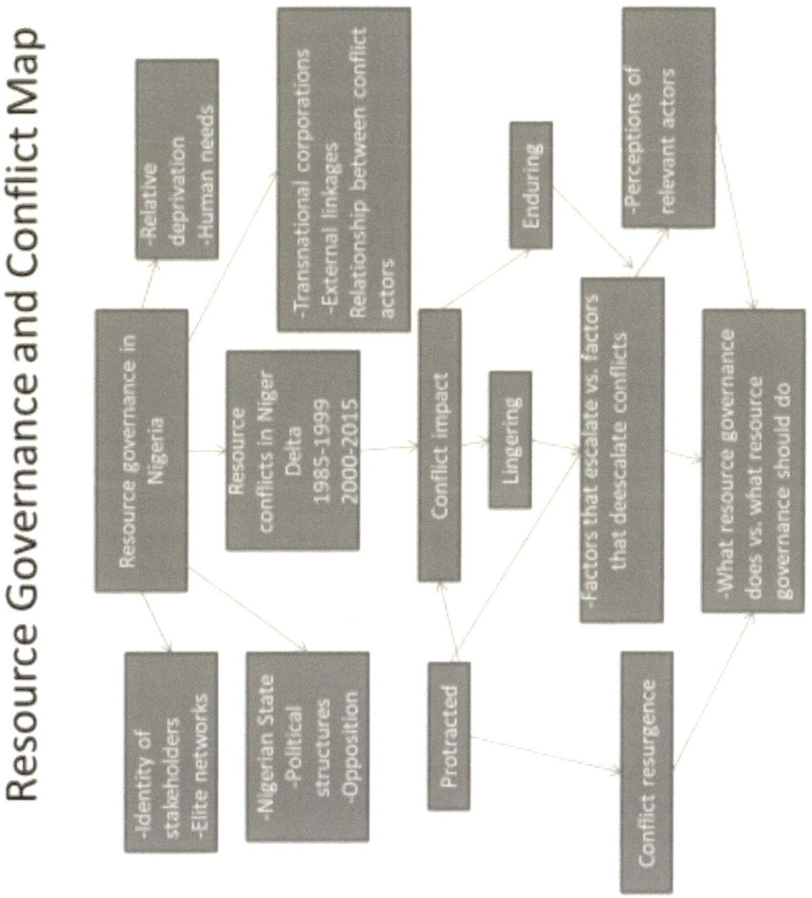

Figure 3.2 Resource Governance and Conflict Map. *Source:* Generated by the author.

structures. To understand resource governance and its impact, it is crucial to examine the identity of stakeholders, elite networks, the Nigerian State, political structures, the opposition, human needs, transnational corporations in the oil industry, external linkages, and the relationship between conflict actors. This inquiry focuses on investigating factors that perpetuate oil-related conflicts in the Nigerian federation and the impact of resource governance on these conflicts. This study explored and isolated the factors that escalate versus factors that deescalate conflicts, the perceptions of relevant actors, and to determine what resource governance does versus what resource governance should do to transform the conflicts. Resource governance methodology emerged as a veritable analytical tool that appropriates Azar's theory to aid in the understanding the perennial conflict in the Niger Delta and to provide a pathway to solutions and resolutions. A robust understanding of the linkages between resource governance, the Nigerian State, and protracted conflict is key to initiating the journey to finding solutions to the Niger Delta burden.

The Intersectionality of Resource Governance, the State, and Protracted Conflict

A nuance understanding and appreciation of the Niger Delta burden should entail intensive analysis and evaluation of the outcome of the interlinkages between resource governance, the Nigerian State, and protracted conflict. In this context, the key influential actors, and stakeholders, like the political decision-makers, policy makers, and transnational energy corporations who drive institutional mechanisms in Nigeria's public space, tend to navigate and control the outcome of events to the disadvantage of the people of the Niger Delta.

The Nigerian State is often described as a rentier state, a monocultural economy which derives its funding from collecting rents from transitional oil corporations. Being heavily dependent on oil revenue, Nigeria is susceptible to the vagaries of the international financial system when the prices of crude oil changes in response to demand and supply. This perspective calls attention to the responses of various governments from military dictatorships to democratically elected government that have violently put down the demands and protests of oil-producing communities with little consideration for dialogue, de-escalation, and mitigation, as the demands of the Niger Delta people are viewed as security threats to the sovereignty of the Nigerian federation. The character of the Nigerian State is considered brutal, repressive, unresponsive to the yearnings of the generality of its people, lacks accountability, and prone to corruption.

The protracted nature of the Niger Delta conflict is traceable to the cultural underpinnings of the grievances of the oil-producing communities which border on issues related to livelihood, survival, social justice, fairness, and equity. Fundamentally critical to the agitations of the local people are the cultural and traditional beliefs relating to land ownership, inheritance, and transfer of wealth within families and lineages versus the imposition of the neocolonial state structure on their traditional way of life. These perspectives are discussed extensively in the next several chapters in this work. In the next chapter, I discuss the key components of resource governance that I choose to call the six pillars of resource governance.

Chapter 4

Six Cardinal Pillars of Resource Governance

Through the processes of analyzing common themes, inferences from media reports, information collection from databases, and personal interviews, I argue that resource governance is most impactful on the perpetuation of the Niger Delta conflict. There are salient implications of my findings and key inferences drawn. Underlying aspects of resource governance as exhibited in the Niger Delta could be analyzed in six considerations: land rights, revenue sharing, oil companies versus oil-producing communities, Nigeria's political structure, environmental protection, and absence of social amenities. I chose to refer to these considerations as the six pillars of resource governance.

LAND RIGHTS

The host communities and the entire people of the Niger Delta seem to have a difficult time in accepting the notion that resources found in their land belong to the federal government. This perspective has economic, political, and cultural ramifications and is rooted in the region's history of struggle that I alluded to in chapter 2. Land is communally owned. Ownership of land is held by families and is passed from parents to children and family lineages over the years. There is a clash of orientation in this regard per two important government policies that negate this belief and traditional norm. Nigeria's Land Use Decree of 1978 and the petroleum law of 1969 fully divest the traditional landed property of the people. The land use decree vested power in the governor of a state who thus can declare a citizen's piece of land as government property when oil is discovered. The petroleum decree also vested authority and power in the federal government of Nigeria.

These laws are comparable to the application of eminent domain laws in the United States. The people routinely refer to the injustice they perceive when they lose fiduciary interest in their piece of farmland or water creek immediately after crude oil is found in one's territory. One's land is automatically taken over by the federal government as soon as crude oil is found there. One participant says the Niger Delta people are "a dispossessed people."

In the process of government acquiring the land for oil production, the landowners also lose their livelihood and in some instances are made to move from their traditional villages to make way for the siting of oil facilities and installations. Though compensations are made for crops, they are not enough to maintain lifetime needs of individual farmers. Similarly intriguing to community people is the realization that while they lose ownership of their farmlands some other Nigerian villages that do not have crude oil and gas resources continue to keep ownership of farmlands without any government interference. The people are unable to reconcile this practice that they consider unfair, unjust, and discriminatory.

The feelings of the Niger Delta people on land rights are rooted in traditional beliefs on land ownership, hereditary, self-determination, and local autonomy. Those beliefs indeed are in direct contradiction to the powers of the Nigerian state. The most fervent protagonists of the Niger Delta struggle argue that the Chiefs and peoples of the Niger Delta did not cede their sovereignty to Nigeria at the cessation of British colonialism. They posit that when the British granted independence to Nigeria in 1960, that sovereignty should have reverted to the ethnic nationalities, all of whom were not dominated by ethnic groups in other parts of the new country. This argument goes further to say the precolonial peoples that inhabited the geographical territory now referred to as Nigeria should have negotiated terms of their inclusion in the new country at independence from Britain. And because that was not done, they surmise, the oil and gas resources being exploited in the bowels of the Niger Delta are, in essence, stolen property.

REVENUE SHARING

The sharing of revenue generated by the federation has been a contentious issue in Nigeria's political discourse. With the introduction of the 1999 Constitution (as amended), the revenue allocation formula has been as follows: 52.68 percent to the federal government, 26.72 percent to state governments, and 20.60 percent to local governments with a special 13 percent derivation to oil-producing states.

The Niger Delta people consider this formula as being unfair and a deviation from the precedent. The popular refrain is to point to the 1960 constitution which provided for the regions to retain 50 percent of revenues derived from their territory. This formula was drastically altered by the military government in 1967 during the civil war and derivation principle expunged. A special 2016 investigative report by the *Vanguard Newspaper* concludes that the Niger Delta got no derivation for fourteen years (1967–1981), including the first oil boom era of the 1970s presided over by Generals Yakubu Gowon and Murtala Mohammed/Olusegun Obasanjo military regimes (Ndujihe, 2016).

President Shehu Shagari's administration introduced 1.5 percent derivation when it set up a Presidential Task Force to address the development problems of the Niger Delta in 1980. The Ibrahim Babangida government increased the derivation percentage to 3 percent in 1992 and then it was increased to 13 percent in 1999 following intense agitation by the Niger Delta and a Supreme Court ruling. Saro-Wiwa in an analogy on the 1992 sharing formula compared the fate of the Niger Delta people to a man whose shirt is taken away and given back three buttons.

There continue to be several perspectives to the agitation for increased access to the crude oil resources exploited in the region. The oil-producing states, the Niger Delta states, call for states to control the resources found in their territory and then they pay taxes to the federal government. Some activists and local communities also call for a certain percentage of the revenue derived in the local villages be directly given for the development of those communities and the local government authorities. Some other community leaders advocate that community development committees be given the responsibility to manage the funds allocated to each community.

Revenue sharing remains a major source of conflict and stokes anger and bitterness in the hearts of Niger Delta agitators. Commissions and Ad-hoc Task Forces instituted to review and make recommendations on revenue sharing have erroneously focused on mere percentage of allocations to the three levels of government. Niger Delta activists call for more focus on revenue generation and rewarding the states and local communities that contribute more to the federal treasury. A 2017 report from the Revenue Mobilization Allocation and Fiscal Commission (RMAFC) identified only three viable states, Lagos, Rivers, and Kano that can run their services without funds from the federation account. In similar vein, the *Economic Confidential* stated in a 2017 special report that fourteen states out of the thirty-six would experience financial collapse without federally allocated revenue. Kebbi state's internally generated revenue (IGR) stood at 4.39 billion Naira (Nigerian currency) while its receipt from the federation account was 76 billion Naira or 5.77 percent. Katsina state and Ekiti state had 6 billion of IGR versus 103 billion Naira in federal allocation representing 5.8 percent and 4.9 billion IGR versus 59 billion federal allocation or 8.38 percent, respectively.

Essentially, federal allocations are derived from receipts from the sale of crude oil and natural gas. Most states in Nigeria are receiver states or subsidized states rather than donor states, they take out more than they contribute to the federation account. In traditional federations, donor states pay more in taxes than they receive back in federal funding.

OIL COMPANIES VERSUS OIL-PRODUCING COMMUNITIES RELATIONS

Discontent and restiveness in the Niger Delta have manifested in several ways as identified in the introductory chapter of this book. One of the consistent complaints and a trigger of conflict is the lack of opportunities to participate in the huge oil and gas industry located in their territory. This complaint also extends to employment opportunities and appointments in the federal government. Granted that the oil industry is a specialized one requiring high-level technical skills, capabilities, and specialized expertise, the local Niger Delta communities consistently and across the board complain that the IOCs do not hire their own people even for low-level positions like drivers, security guards, dispatchers, cleaners, messengers, and similar jobs.

Participants in my study and independent observers have pointed out that during the second republic (1979–1983), the civilian state governments in the Niger Delta attempted to implement a joint policy of requiring IOCs operating in their domains to reserve the hiring of employees on salary grade scale of 01-06 for the indigenes of the state. While there was a general acknowledgment that it was a commendable and feasible proposal, the IOCs pushed back arguing that oil and gas resources are exclusively matters only the federal government could legislate upon by constitutional provisions.

There are also complaints that the local people have no opportunities to own any portion of these giant multinational corporations with huge capital outlay. The IOCs enter into operational agreements with the federal government only. The local communities, local authorities, and state governments have virtually no input.

One controversial perspective of this complaint concerns the allegation that oil mining licenses and oil lifting contracts are exclusively given to persons from non-oil-producing areas of Nigeria to the disadvantage of citizens on whose territory oil and gas resources are found. Indeed, a candidate for governor in Bayelsa in 2015 used this as a major issue in his campaigns as alluded to in chapter 1 of this book. Niger Delta advocates argue that these unfair practices occur and persist because the dominant ethnic groups in the country—the Hausa-Fulani, Yoruba, and the Igbos—are the ones who oversee decision-making both within the government and the IOCs.

The Petroleum Industry Governance Bill (PIGB) has stagnated in the National Assembly for a decade with iterations. The bill gave a prospect of given oil-producing communities 10 percent equity shares in the prospecting company or 10 percent ownership of the oil and gas produced in their domain. The local people had looked forward with the hope of the day they would be part owners of the crude. But it was not to be.

Given the foregoing, I can conclude that the theoretical positions of Azar in the PSC model hold true in the case of the Niger Delta. Azar's argument that communities being deprived of satisfaction of their basic needs, based on their identity, is the result of "a complex causal chain involving the role of the state and the pattern of international linkages" is applicable to the oil-producing communities in the Niger Delta. The structural character of the Nigerian state mirrors the conception of Azar in the third step of his four-step theory; the state apparatus is dominated by a few prevailing communal groups, Hausa-Fulani, Yoruba, and Ibo who manage and allocate Nigeria's oil resources for their own self-interest and benefits much to the frustration of the minority groups, the oil-producing communities, in the Niger Delta.

Oil-producing communities vent their anger at oil companies because they see IOCs and government as one and the same. To the reckoning of the host communities, Shell Oil, Chevron, Agip, or other oil companies are symbols of the government. For these communities, there is no sign of government in their midst. There are no government projects, programs, or activity. There is virtually no government presence in most of these communities. In the thinking of the local people, the IOCs are the government. The IOCs are the only way to get to the government. The federal government capital is Abuja, 500 miles away. Even though there are two other tiers of government, namely, the state governments and local governments beside the federal government, the impact of those other tiers of government on the oil-producing communities have been minimal or completely non-existent. There have also been concerns that corruption and misappropriation of funds accruing to the other levels of government have contributed to lack of development in the Niger Delta communities. Before Abuja was built Lagos was Nigeria's capital city located some 390 miles away.

Nigeria's monocultural economy is dominated by transnational oil and gas companies given their contributions to the gross domestic product and federal revenue, including foreign exchange earnings. Besides the domineering role of transnational oil companies in the Nigerian economy, the oil-producing communities feel almost total powerlessness relative to the activities of the

IOCs in their local communities combined with the use of state power by the federal government to suppress their agitations and deny them rights to the natural resources found in their land. No matter how united and better organized, the local oil-producing communities are no match for the collaboration and coordination between the oil companies and the security agents of the federal government in any confrontation. This realization triggers and perpetuates the feelings of deprivation, unfairness, and social injustice in the citizens of the Niger Delta.

A community chief, participant Nanga588, reflects on the agony he faces when oil company officials waive a letter of authority obtained from a government official in Abuja to conduct oil production without any input or consultation with local people:

> Let me explain what the multinational oil companies do to the owners of the natural resources in our land. They obtain a piece of paper from the government in Lagos and take the paper and go to Ogoni and destroy the environment, spill oil into the creeks of the delta people, and when the people raise an issue, you say, they are terrorists. And the man who gave you this piece of paper would now come with a gun and put a gun to your head. So, it is the multinational companies that are at the core of the conflicts.[1]
>
> The above sentiments are widespread and held by a large section of people in the Niger Delta. Provisions of the Land Use Decree of 1978 and Petroleum Decree of 1969, which have been revised and included in the 1999 Constitution (as amended), transfer ownership of lands, creeks, streams, and watercourses to the federal government when crude oil and gas and minerals are found in commercial quantities. These constitutional provisions along with Oil Pipelines Act, 1990 expropriate the right of action by a landowner on whose land crude oil and gas deposits are found. The oil company with an oil pipeline permit holder is only required to give 14-day notice to the occupier of the land before entering same and to pay compensation for crops, trees, and gardens damaged. My findings show that landowners not only lose title to their farmlands, creeks, and waterways, they are also shortchanged when they seek compensation. The process of attaching value to crops, trees, and gardens are wholly controlled by the oil companies. Granted that social responsibility programs have been initiated by some of the IOCs in a handful of oil-producing communities, the efforts are voluntary and not required by law. And they pale in significance with the wealth being appropriated by the IOCs from the crude oil and gas in their environment.

Based on the preceding discussion, I conclude that my research confirms the position of Azar concerning the role of international linkages to conflicts.

The IOCs operating in the Niger Delta are key players in conflict and must be involved in an effort aimed at transforming the conflict.

ENVIRONMENTAL POLLUTION

One of the most vociferous grievances of the people of the Niger Delta remains the environmental pollution caused by the oil production and exploration activities of IOCs in the region. The concerns for environmental remediation in the Niger Delta have attracted national and international attention. The oil industry started way before Nigeria secured independence from Britain and robust environmental measures were not put in place to guide the IOCs operating in the region.

The Nigerian government in 2009 invited United Nations Environment Program (UNEP) to do an assessment of oil pollution in Ogoniland in response to the agitation of the Ogoni people against Shell Oil. In 2011, UNEP released a report on environment damage caused in Ogoniland in the Niger Delta due to the oil and gas exploration activities of Shell Oil. The report says because of the severity of the pollution it would take thirty years to clean up the environment and recommended an initial provision of $1 billion to be paid by the Nigerian government and all IOCs to fund the clean-up.

The study found high concentration of hydrocarbon and benzene, two carcinogens, in high concentration in outdoor air and drinking water in Ogoniland. In Ogale, in Eleme local government area (LGA) some contaminated wells were found to be contaminated by benzene at over 900 times above the World Health Organization guideline. In addition, water samples taken from at least seven wells near the NNPC pipelines in the town were found to contain hydrocarbon at least 1,000 times above the Nigerian drinking water standard of three micrograms per liter. The UNEP team stated that in many of the locations, there was contamination of ground water that constituted serious threat to human health and the viability and productivity of the ecosystem. The non-implementation of the recommendations of the report, some of which were supposed to be treated with urgency, appears to add to the discontent and frustration with the government.

Gas flares have caused significant climate change in the Niger Delta. The ecosystem has been tremendously altered with mangrove trees being replaced by nipa palms and seaweed. Acid rain (the black rain) causes soothe and damages the zinc roof, and most homeowners are forced to take on additional expense of changing roofs every two years. Gas flares cause intensive and persistent noise pollution in villages close to oil fields and other oil facilities. The IOCs recklessly lay pipelines within villages and close to homes and dwellings with the risk of explosions and leaks. Besides the poor operations practices of IOCs, the response or lack thereof of IOCs to oil spills, pipeline explosions, and leaks has miffed and escalated the strain relationship with oil companies and the oil-producing communities. Some of the pipelines were laid for decades and corrosion and wear and tear do set in to cause explosions, spills, and pollution.

When oil spills occur, the IOCs would hardly ever take any responsibility. When community leaders demand restitution and mitigation the IOCs would rather use their enormous financial resources to hire top-rated lawyers to fight the communities in courts for decades than pay the appropriate compensation. Communities from Bodo in Ogoni area engaged in litigation with Shell Oil for several years both in Nigerian and international courts over allegations that oil spills from pipelines destroyed farmlands, crops, and waterways.

ABSENCE OF SOCIAL AMENITIES

Most of the oil-producing communities in the Niger Delta are in difficult terrain and lack basic social amenities like electricity, pipe-borne water, hospitals, and well-equipped schools. The realization that crude oil resources from the region has helped build major cities and provided comfort, opportunities, and social infrastructure to other non-producing regions triggers anger and bitterness among the people. As indicated in chapter 5, several host communities staged several protests concerning non-provision of basic amenities by IOCs operating in their communities.

The foregoing analysis upholds and confirms the literature on resource governance. As Alao (2007) states, "it is the failure of the states to effectively integrate all the contents of resource governance that is at the root of conflicts" (p. 35).

NIGERIA'S POLITICAL STRUCTURE

Nigeria's political structure appears to be tilted against the people of the Niger Delta. Even though Nigeria runs a federal government, the country's political structure appears to favor the dominant groups as perceived by the people in the region. Before 1978 when the Land Use Decree was promulgated by the military government, oil companies either paid annual rent to the landowners for the use of their land or purchased a plot of land for their use (Frynas, 2001). The 1978 Land Use Decree redefined the legal position of land ownership in Nigeria by vesting the ownership of all land within the state in the state governor. Since 1978, therefore, the IOCs pay rents for land acquired for oil production to the state governor and not the landowners in the host communities. This is a key root of disaffection and discontent in the oil-bearing communities. This decree and many other ones issued by the military hierarchy during the period of military rule has since been ratified as acts of the legislature.

To make changes to these laws requires two-thirds majority votes in the National Assembly and two-thirds of the state assemblies to overturn the decrees that were issued by the military governments and made part of the substantive laws of the country. Some have argued that if the oil and gas resources were in the territory of the dominant groups that the derivation principle should still have been retained and that the complaints of the oil-producing communities would have been addressed.

Niger Delta activists argue that the several times the county was divided into more states, took away from the resources of the people of the Niger Delta. They argue that some of the states are not economically viable, that the states depend on the funds allocated to them from the federal purse, revenue the majority of which is derived from crude oil sales. They argue that in 1967, there were three oil-producing states in the Niger Delta and thus received one-fourth or 25 percent of total federal revenue or 3/12, as there were twelve states in the country. Since 1996 Nigeria has thirty-six states and with six Niger Delta states, thus the Niger Delta states now receive 16 percent of the federal revenue or 6/36 or one-sixth.

The following quote attributed to the highest-ranking bureaucrat in the Ministry of Mines and Power, Lagos, in 1980 is often cited by Niger Delta analysts as evidence that Nigeria's political structure is unfavorable to their interests:

> Like [*sic*] in many other areas of the world, the regions where oil is found in this country are very inhospitable. They are mainly in swamps and creeks. They require massive injection of money if their conditions and standards of living are to compare with what attains elsewhere in the country where possibilities of agriculture and diversified industry are much greater. There is a nudging acceptance of the special needs of oil areas in the latest proposals being discussed by the government, but I believe there is a long way to go to meet the claims of the oil-producing areas which see themselves losing non-replaceable resources while replaceable and permanent resources of agriculture and industry are being developed elsewhere largely with oil revenue. Given, however, the small size and population of oil-producing areas, it is not cynical to observe that even if the resentments of oil producing states continue, they cannot threaten the stability of the country nor affect its continued economic development.[2]

Another issue of grievance is what Niger Delta agitators call the unjust and unfair allocation of oil mining licenses to persons from non-producing areas outside the Niger Delta. The point being raised here is that those who control political power call the shots and that it is a difficult task to change or influence government policy to one's favor if one lacks the political leverage.

It is critical to emphasize, even though it has been tangentially stated in this study, that the collective impact of the decades of military rule in Nigeria whereby profound policy decisions that significantly alter the fate millions of citizens were made by proclamations, military decrees, and edicts made by a handful of military brass has entrenched in the political system unfair, unjust, and cruel mechanisms that seem to have caused tremendous disadvantages to the people of the Niger Delta. One important example that requires extensive discussion is the handling of solid minerals versus oil and gas by the Nigerian government. Whereas the ownership of crude oil and natural gas is exclusively vested in the federal government, the development, exploitation, and extraction of other solid minerals such as bitumen, gold, diamond, uranium, titanium, and marble are extended to state governments, and private investors.

The arguments in this finding align with the theoretical position of Azar in his PSC model that where there is collective communal identity and dominant groups control political power and the distribution of resources, the dominant groups tend to corner the resources to the exclusion of the numerically smaller groups leading to conflict.

I have shown in the foregoing sections that resource governance constitutes the most significant impact on the manifestation of resource conflicts in Nigeria's Niger Delta by discussing the six pillars of resource governance. Drawing on the dominant themes in my data, direct comments, and opinions of participants interviewed in the field in the Niger Delta, and the comments in literature on my research topic, I can reach the conclusion that my findings answer my central research, how does resource governance impact protracted resource conflicts in Nigeria's Niger Delta? Most of the issues and topics analyzed as impacting conflicts in the Niger Delta emanate from and revolve around resource governance. Next, I discuss the grievances of the people of the Niger Delta, "In the Eyes of the People."

NOTES

1. Personal interview, Amasoma, Bayelsa State, Nigeria, December 2017.
2. This statement is an attachment to the Ogoni Bill of Rights, 1990, a publication of the Movement for the Survival of the Ogoni People (MOSOP), Nigeria.

Chapter 5

In the Eyes of the People

Perceptions and Grievances

The key finding in my study suggests that resource governance is at both the heart of conflict and the ideal place to seek solutions. Conflict actors, conflict management agents, and those interested in understanding and proffering solutions to the Niger Delta conflict would need to channel resources to the complex nature of resource governance and its impact on conflict in the region. In the following sections, I examine specific grievances and perspectives of the oil-producing communities.

DATA FROM NIGERIA WATCH AND OTHER CONFLICT/VIOLENCE DATABASES

In this section, I chose to focus only on data from Nigeria Watch given their unique relevance to my work. A review of identified databases on the Niger Delta reveals the following patterns:

- 2009 was the most turbulent year in terms of fatalities/confrontation of militant groups such as MEND against IOCs. Nigeria Watch database shows that IOCs are a major factor in the intensity/escalation of lethal violence. The IOCs as a routine practice invite the army, police, and other highly specialized state security personnel to protect their employees and facilities whenever a dispute arises with the host communities or when they feel threatened.
- Shell, ExxonMobil, and Chevron are the major players in Nigeria (listed in the Fortune Global 500 of the world's largest companies) (Hassan, 2013, 239).

- To many observers, the oil industry in Nigeria is thus associated with disasters, violence, oil spills, pollution, and vandalism. Economic issues, like oil production, are the fifth main cause of violence in the country. The other four causes of violence include the deployment of soldiers for law enforcement and security operations, the confrontation of the Army and Boko Haram Islamic militants, excessive use of force by the police in engagement with civilians, and the clashes of the security services and political groups (Afeno, 2014).
- Oil is a human security issue. Between 2006 and 2014, a total of 1,547 and 4,548 victims died nationwide in incidents related, respectively, to violence in oil production and distribution.
- To understand incidents of conflict and violence in the oil industry, in the Niger Delta, a distinction must be made between the upstream sector (i.e., exploration and production), and the downstream sector (i.e., marketing and distribution). IOCs that have more offshore operations have lower incidents of violence/conflict encounters and thus lower fatalities. In onshore production, there are obviously many more actors involved in violence. The youth, insurgents, women, and development associations of host communities are involved in resisting oil exploration and production. There are much more incidents of these groups confronting state security agents.
- The core oil-producing areas in the Niger Delta recorded the highest number of violent deaths related to the petroleum industry in the upstream sector, with Delta State as the most affected with 770 deaths followed by Rivers State with 700 deaths between 2006 and 2014.
- The use of security forces by the government often exacerbates the problem (i.e., conflict) with the deployment of troops, gunboats, and helicopters. Whether it has been invited by oil companies to intervene or not, the army is notoriously brutal. In May 2009, for instance, the bombardment of seven communities in Gbaramatu kingdom in Warri South West LGA, Delta State, suspected of harboring militant camps, led to the death of well over 500 people (Afeno, 2014, 29).
- When the women of Gbaramatu and Egbema clans in Warri South West LGA in the Delta State took over Chevron-Texaco flow stations on July 15, 2002, they gave the reasons for their protests as ecological damage, unemployment, and lack of social amenities (Ezeilo, 2007).

As shown in Table 5.1, key issues of concern that trigger and escalate the conflicts in the region are summarized under resource control, the handling of the situation of the Ogoni people, resource ownership, land rights, revenue allocation/revenue allocation formula, the derivation principle in revenue sharing, and environmental pollution. In ranking order, other important issues include absence of social amenities, perceived neglect by government and the

Table 5.1 Topics Discussed in the Press on the Niger Delta Conflicts 2007–2017

Topics Rank	*Percentage (%)*
Resource control	9.16
Ogoni crisis	8.54
Resource ownership/land rights	7.91
Revenue allocation/revenue allocation formula	7.70
Derivation principle	7.30
Environmental pollution/clean-up	7.08
Militancy/amnesty	6.45
Restructuring of federation	5.83
Absence of social amenities	5.20
Lack of development/government /TNC neglect	5.00
Oil mining/oil lifting licenses/federal appointments/employment	4.58
Kidnapping/ransoming of oil workers/attacks on oil facilities	4.16
Transnational oil companies/community elations	3.95
Oil mining licenses/oil lifting contracts	3.54
Sovereign national conference	3.12
Violence/killings/cultism/insecurity	2.91
Human rights abuses/social injustice	2.29
Illegal oil bunkering/local refineries	2.08
Offshore/onshore oil wells	1.66
States creation/more local governments/other	1.45

Source: Data generated by the author from NIIA research collection.

IOCs, unemployment, and lack of access to contracts in the oil industry and government appointments. I expatiate on these key issues in chapter 6.

Next, I turn my attention to review, discuss, and analyze in greater detail the specific responses of participants I interviewed in the field. I conducted interviews in Port Harcourt in Rivers State and Yenegoa in Bayelsa, Nigeria, during November and December 2017. A total of thirty participants were interviewed including opinion experts knowledgeable about natural resource conflicts and the Niger Delta, a good diversity of men, women, chiefs, NGO leaders, university scholars, political leaders, activists, youths, ex-militants, and community leaders.[1]

DEEPENING MY ENQUIRIES

My main research question is, how does resource governance impact enduring resource conflicts in Nigeria's Niger Delta? The subsidiary questions were—what are the identities and agendas of stakeholders, and networks in the Niger Delta conflicts; how does perception of relative deprivation of human needs contribute to the persistence of the conflicts; what roles do Nigeria's political structures play in the emergence, sustenance, and resurgence of resource conflicts? In what ways do mobilization methods of conflict actors affect the relationship between transnational oil corporations and oil-producing communities?

To obtain data and to find explanations to my main research question and the subsidiary research questions, I posed several questions in semi-structured interviews. During the pre-interview introduction, the participants were made familiar with the working definition of resource governance, as used in this study:

> Resource governance refers to all the internal and external considerations that come to play in the management of natural resources. These considerations include domestic laws, constitutional provisions, cultural practices, customary laws, neo-patrimonial practices, and all international treaties and obligations that govern such issues as the ownership, extraction, management, and sharing of natural resources within a given country.

1. *In understanding the Niger Delta conflicts, how significant is resource governance? What do you perceive to be the impact of resource governance on the conflicts in the Niger Delta? Please give some examples of positive and negative impact.*

Most of the participants are of the view that resource governance is the most significant element in understanding and managing conflicts in the Niger Delta. And that resource governance is at the root of the protracted resource conflicts in Nigeria's Niger Delta. A total of 96.67 percent of participants suggest that resource governance had the most impact on the nature of conflicts in the region. In other words, twenty-nine of the thirty interviewees propose that the crux of the protracted conflicts is embedded in resource governance. An independent researcher on security matters in the civil society community, participant Alale310, for example, states, "Resource governance, especially, resource ownership, is the most important issue critical to resolving the Niger Delta conflicts."[2] Considering the overwhelming number of the participants who identify resource governance as the crux of the conflicts and the suggestion that the resource ownership is the most critical issue to resolving them, it means that my study must, of necessity, pay close attention and reflect on these perspectives in my analysis and conclusions. I discuss this all-important point in chapter 6 under the findings section especially as it relates to the literature.

Another respondent, a university teacher in Port Harcourt who grew up in the oil-producing community of Botem Tai in the Tai LGA, had similar sentiments. University lecturer Prof. Dogo820 states,

> I would say that natural resource governance is pivotal to resolving the issues of conflicts in the region, intra communal conflicts, and inter-communal

> conflicts, conflicts between the communities and the oil industry which is very pronounced in the region, conflicts between the Nigerian state and the people of this region . . . there is always the agitation for resource control in this region because the people feel that the resources that are found in this region are not used for the benefits of the people of this region.[3]

This observation from a university scholar raises several issues at the same time. First, it identifies layers of conflict—the Nigerian state versus the people of the Niger Delta, conflict between the oil-producing communities and the transnational oil companies, inter-communal conflicts, and intra-communal conflicts. In addition, the scholar's observation embraces perceptions, grievances, and alleges that resources explored in the region are not used for the benefits of its peoples. This is important for my study as one of my key objectives is to understand the perceptions of stakeholders regarding the sharing of proceeds from crude oil production.

Most participants, twenty-four out of thirty, or 80 percent, aver that resource governance has a crucial impact on the environment, on the means of livelihood, in the Niger Delta both at the national level and the local levels. From the point of view of the local people, the people traditionally depend solely on fishing and farming as their occupations. The local people of the Niger Delta get their biodiversity resources from the environment to survive, the same environment where oil and gas resources are found.

Oil and gas operations have caused community leaders to raise concerns about environmental pollution and other forms of environmental degradation. These environmental issues, participants say, impact directly on the livelihood support system of the people. Environmental concerns are said to be major sources of conflict. Resource governance is critically crucial in the whole value system in terms of the enabling laws that conserve or fail to conserve the natural environment of the people or whether or not the laws make provisions for compensation when people lose their livelihood support structures.

One participant observed that the Nigerian oil and gas industry started in colonial times, as already indicated in chapter 2, which discusses the background and historical context of this work, when the country did not have robust environmental conservation laws. And that the environmental impact assessment law, for example, only came into being in Nigeria in 1992 after the Koko toxic dump of June 1988. To give a little context, the Koko toxic dump refers to an incident where two Italian ships dumped industrial wastes from Europe in a sleepy coastal village of Koko in the Warri North LGA in Edo State. The industrial wastes caused severe ecological damage to the creeks, aquatic life, mangrove forests, and farmlands in Koko and surrounding villages. There was a huge outcry from the community, local activists, the media, and the state government at the time. Participant Zima450 asserts,

> Environmental impact assessment is very crucial in resource governance all over the world because it tends to identify negative factors in proposed new development in order to proffer mitigation measures. . . . Nigeria's environmental impact assessment law emerged about three decades after the oil industry was already here. And so, there was no such impact analysis to guide the operations and the siting of the structures in the region.[4]

The impact of decades of oil production on the local farmers and fishermen and fisherwomen in the Niger Delta is referenced by several participants throughout the interviews irrespective of the location of the participants. This renewed focus on the environment is timely for this study given that during the months I did my fieldwork, there was a renewed media attention on the UNEP proposal to clean up environmental pollution sites in the Ogoni area of Rivers State by the federal government. This is a critical perspective to literature, given that the perspective of participants hints at both preventative and mitigative benefits of policy measures targeting the needs of the oil-producing communities.

One example of positive impact identified by participants is the increase of derivation principle in the revenue sharing formula from 1.5 percent to 13 percent in 1999. Five participants or 16.66 percent of respondents point out that this was due to pressure and the agitation of the oil-producing communities and only came after the oil-producing states and Lagos took the federal government to the Supreme Court. The highest court of the land ruled in favor of the plaintiffs. The court decision resulted in the oil-producing states receiving additional 117.9 million Naira (Nigeria's currency) in derivation funds out of the total crude oil earnings of 7.815 billion Naira in fiscal year 1982 (Ndujihe, 2016). The participants who subscribe to this view are quick to add that this policy measure did not go far enough.

Identifying a positive impact by participants in the midst of a litany of grievances, negative perceptions, and allegations of government neglect, for this research, provides an opening that could be exploited by conflict resolution agents and the government to discuss and provide options for peace or resolution, a potential contribution to literature.

The second example of a positive impact in terms of government policy is the introduction of the NDDC by the Obasanjo administration. The objective of the NDDC is broadly similar to that of the NDBDB that was set up by the colonial administration in 1958 to address the development needs and terrain of the region "because of the problems of development in this area of creeks and mangrove." The NDBDB initiative occurred before crude oil became the major revenue source for the Nigerian government. I discussed this in detail in chapter 2.

Most participants suggest that the perception of the people had been that this was a welcome policy given the lofty objectives of the body. Some participants, however, expressed concerns regarding the performance of the agency, an issue discussed later in this study. Most participants suggest that the initiation of credible policies aimed at addressing the grievances of the people would go a long way to deescalate the conflicts in the region. For instance, twenty-four of the thirty interviews or 80 percent of participants subscribe to this view. This is a significant finding because it means that there is hope that if the views of the participants are collated and reflected in the recommendations, and government policies are targeted to address them, there is a likelihood that such would help to deescalate the conflicts.

Most participants assert that persistent calls for the restructuring of Nigeria's federal structure, protests in the Niger Delta, kidnapping of oil workers, attacks on oil infrastructures, and the filing of lawsuits against the federal government and the transnational oil companies are the manifestations of the negative impact of resource governance. 86.67 percent of, or twenty-six of thirty, respondents conclude that the government's failure to study, understand, and to set up appropriate and comprehensive policy mechanisms to address the complex issues embedded in the grievances of the people of the Niger Delta over the last couple of decades is a negative outcome of resource governance.

2. *Who do you consider to be the critical actors, stakeholders, agendas, and networks in the Niger Delta conflicts? Identify and give specific examples. Any change in the identity and influence of these actors and networks during the span of the conflicts?*

All the participants, that is thirty out of thirty, or 100 percent, identify three critical layers of actors in the conflicts in the Niger Delta. These are the government, the international oil companies, and the oil-producing communities. These actors are considered the primary actors. So, you have the federal government of Nigeria with its capital in Abuja, and IOCs like Shell, Mobil, Chevron, Agip, Total, and Panocean. Other subsidiary stakeholders mentioned include oil marketers, oil servicing companies, holders of oil lifting licenses, security agencies that protect the oil companies and their facilities, and community groups like CBOs and religious organizations.

The subsidiary actors are further subdivided into community networks and business networks. Community networks include traditional rulers, women's groups, youth groups, and families and lineages. Some of these youth groups are composed of cult groups, gangs, and militants; some are unarmed, and others are peaceful. One participant Pastor Albert530 who wears many hats—a son of a traditional ruler, a pastor, and community activist—suggests that families within host communities must be considered as key actors, for according to this participant, land ownership belongs to families and groups of families. Land is directly owned by families. Business networks include oil lifting licensees, oil marketers, contractors, agents, trade unions, oil servicing groups, and transportation companies. Using his community as an example, participant Pastor Albert530 says families are direct owners of the land where oil wells are located and should be consulted and carried along when decisions are being made on oil and gas matters by the government, IOCs, and the local community. The exclusion of families in the decision-making process is, according to this participant, a persistent source of conflict.

For this inquiry, two significant informal networks were observed—the first is an alliance between the top hierarchy of security agents deployed to protect pipelines and oil industry infrastructure and elements of networks engaged in oil bunkering. Bunkering is a term used to describe the process of filling a ship or tanker with oil or coal. Illegal oil bunkering is therefore a fancy name for crude oil theft. Illegal oil bunkers forge documents and signatures of approving naval personnel and government officials and move crude oil outside the shores of Nigeria and sell them on the world markets. The unsold crude oil is refined at illegal, private local refineries, which produce gasoline, kerosene, and diesel fuel. Oil industry watchers warn that these local refineries cause environment damage. As indicated earlier above, environmental impact of oil production is a major concern in all the oil-producing communities, and it is critical for this study to isolate the specifics of those grievances related to pollution.

A second informal network flourishes whereby the operatives of the state security network have infiltrated the ranks and co-opted some elements within the militant groups to counter their activities. This is a government policy of inducements, settlement, and co-optation which is said to have led to the weakening of the many militant groups. Participant Chief102, already cited above, says some of the militant groups have been so compromised that they provide intelligence on the activities of their fellow militant groups to the authorities. This alleged collaboration assists the government to crush the insurgency from time to time.

On the question about change in the identity and influence of actors, there have been significant changes in four key aspects. One, the leading voices in the agitation have shifted from educated and mature intellectuals like Saro-Wiwa to mostly much younger, less educated, inexperienced but equally passionate elements.

Second, whereas the Niger Delta struggle originally started with the Ogoni people in Rivers State, as stated earlier in this study, it has attracted adherents in several other communities in several states in the region, during the last two decades, such that advocates are now also found in Akwa Ibom, Bayelsa, Cross River, Delta, and Edo States. Indeed, the communities whose terrain is more riverine and difficult to access in terms of transportation, seem to be better launching pads and campsites for the militants.

Third, the leading actors could be publicly identified and held accountable during the first few years of the agitation. In the current dispensation, the contemporary generation of actors, for the most part, operate underground, and publicly identify themselves using aliases or nicknames. This could be attributable to the potential threats of arrest or imprisonment from the security forces.

Fourth, most actors are now armed and adopt violent methods of agitation as opposed to the first decade where peaceful and nonviolent methods of agitation held sway.

Fifth, there has been significant changes among the security apparatuses of government, the IOCs, and the armed groups agitating on behalf of the local oil-producing communities. Government and the IOCs have devoted more financial resources, personnel, and logistics to quell the conflicts in the region. The government permanently keeps units of all specializations in Nigeria's armed forces, a coalition of the Army, Air Force, Navy, Police Mobile Force, and the officers from the State Security Service in the Niger Delta to put down any violent protests and agitations. These special security outfits and their operations are given codenames. At the time of my fieldwork, during November and December 2017, the government had "Operation Crocodile Smile" in action in the Niger Delta. Some participants, for examples, Opuko870, Alale310, and Nolee210, point to a closer coordination between the state security apparatuses and the security departments of the IOCs. This observation can only be collaborated by those who have privileged knowledge like those who are themselves security agents or current or ex-militants. A few of the participants claim to have personal experiences in these matters. To ensure the accuracy and authenticity of this information I had to corroborate information from two or more other participants.

As indicated above, youths of Niger Delta now also engage in illegal bunkering to earn an income and participate in tasting the commodity that belches from their homeland and has been used to build Abuja, Nigeria's capital city, and other regions in the country. Twenty years ago, this practice was unimaginable. The observed changes in the identities and influence of conflict actors in the Niger Delta are important contributions of this study to the literature on protracted conflict. Whereas the existing literature discusses "elite networks," the changes observed are rather within the grassroots, outside of elite platforms.

Several reasons were given for the changes. First, participants say the government has responded with large-scale violence to the demands of the Niger Delta people. One respondent, Opuko870, quoted earlier, stated that during an arranged visit to a militant camp, the militants gave one of the reasons for choosing to bear arm was because they "did not want to die like Saro-Wiwa." According to them, the militants, Saro-Wiwa chose the path of nonviolence and peaceful struggle and he was killed by the government. They argued that they would rather die fighting than agitate peacefully and be killed by Nigerian security forces. Here is the relevant portion of the opinion of Opuko870, an Ogoni community leader:

> In those days during the height of the violence, of militancy in the Niger Delta by armed gangs and militias, I am talking about, 2007, 2008, and part of 2009, when you visited some of the military camps, if you visit some of those camps, the militants, the armed gangs were saying that they did not want to die like Saro-Wiwa.[5]

Such comments have also been expressed by other Niger Delta advocates mostly in frustration over the use of heavy state violence to put down peaceful protests or public demonstrations by oil-producing communities. What this means for this study is that it is important to isolate why and when this change of heart takes place, especially among the youth of the Niger Delta. The implication for this research is that youth, broadly speaking, are the driving force regarding the course and nature of the struggle in the Nigeria Delta. The youth are the ones who, for the most part, repeatedly complain about unemployment, lack of opportunities, and absence of social amenities.

Second, some of the participants, eighteen out of thirty respondents, or 60 percent, suggest that the government tend to respond swiftly and positively to violent attacks than to peaceful protests. Participant Chief Nelson562 suggests that the Nigerian government based in Abuja is not actually interested in the resolution of the Niger Delta crisis. And that the government is only interested in the oil and the income accruing to it, as according to the participant's reckoning, the government's goal is that crude oil should continue to flow. Alluding to the rise of the Niger Delta Avengers [NDA] in 2016, the participant asserts that when the Niger Delta Avengers started their attacks on oil facilities, what the National Security Adviser's office did was to gather some of the so-called ex-militant leaders, funded them, and especially most of those who were sympathetic to the APC [All Progressives Congress] government to also provide intelligence and information from the villages and creeks to the security agencies so that the security agencies could attack the bases of the Avengers. Another participant, Zima450, expresses similar view on the response of the government arguing that there are two scenarios to reflect on the method of struggle and the response of the government—the nonviolent approach that was adopted by the Ogoni in the early days and the present-day approach, that is the violent approach adopted by the other part of the Niger Delta, the Ijaws. Participants surmise that over the years, the use of violent approach attracts quick attention by the government, whereas the nonviolent approach is often neglected and underappreciated and underrated by the government and the oil companies. The contention is that there is a history, a consistent pattern whereby the violent approach is attractive in terms of getting responses from the international oil companies and the government even though the violent approach is costly in terms of human lives and the violations, and to a large extent, the infringement on the rights of the people that the struggle was intended to protect. Participants, for example, observe that there are scenarios whereby violent, armed militant agitators in the Niger Delta, apart from vandalizing oil installations also rape women, also adopt violent approaches that would lead to the death of their own people.

> The other scenario shows the nonviolent approach, that does not present the same type of internal abuse of the rights of the people but in terms of response, or seemingly proactive response to the agitations, the government, and the oil companies respond faster, quicker to violent agitations than nonviolent agitations. It is very unfortunate.[6]

Third, some respondents, nine out of thirty, or 26.27 percent, claim that the government and the IOCs have not been honest, transparent, and accountable during their discussions with the people of the Niger Delta. All this, they contend, has engendered a sense of distrust of government and the IOCs. One respondent, Alale310, who claimed to have acted as a go-between, as a negotiator during a kidnapping episode, suggested that the distrust of the government and IOCs in some Niger Delta communities was so high that sometimes, members of CSOs with good intentions who offered to approach the communities on behalf on the government were not welcome, given their past experiences. An excerpt of participant Alale310's observation is appropriate here:

> For some time, I have been saying that the reason why you see the communities embroiled in crisis is also because they have seen, over the years, how the community people have many times, been short-changed by the government and the oil companies. When anyone comes around to do anything, even with all the good intention, they see you as a part of that team, as part of the oppressors that have come to short-change them too.[7]

Some of the respondents, nine out of thirty, or 30 percent, point to a conflict of interest regarding the Nigerian government being both an investor and a protector of the oil industry and considers this a conflict trigger. Participant Zima450, for example, argues,

Unfortunately, the Nigerian government is both an investor and a protector, which is a conflict of interest. You cannot be an investor in the business of oil production and at the same time you are saddled with the responsibility of ensuring that the entire value chain of oil and gas production in the country is done in a credible and transparent manner. No, it will not work.[8]

This participant's concern is at the core of the conflict in the Niger Delta as the reference is to the business relationship the Nigerian government has with the IOCs operating in the region. The government enters into a contract agreement with the IOCs such that the predominant contract model for exploration, development, and production of Nigeria's hydrocarbon resources is the joint venture (JV) arrangement, under which the government, acting through the state hydrocarbon company (NNPC), contributes substantial counterpart funding (cash calls) to meet equity participation in the JV, in which the state holds majority shares. The Nigerian government has 60 percent equity in these JV agreements except for Shell Oil where it has 55 percent. The bulk of Nigerian crude oil production is shared between the production sharing contracts (PSCs) and the JV licenses, while service contracts, sole risk contracts, and marginal field licenses make up a minuscule, at most 5 percent collectively. The host communities, the oil-producing villages, and citizens of the Niger Delta are not and have never been involved in the complex, financial, and technical decisions, or any decisions about these agreements.

3. *What is your take on the grievances of the Niger Delta communities? 4. How do human needs and perception of relative deprivation come into play in discussing resource conflicts in the Niger Delta region?*

On the twin issues of human needs and perception of relative deprivation, most participants, twenty-seven out of thirty, or 90 percent, suggest that the oil and gas resources found in their territory belong to the local people and that the people have this sense of injustice being done to them when the national government takes away the proceeds of oil production and fails to provide to them any infrastructure, development projects, social programs, or benefits. And that over the years, this realization has instilled in the people a sense of anger, bitterness, and frustration. In discussing resource conflicts in the Niger Delta, therefore, this is a recurrent refrain. Any measures being considered to manage the conflicts must, of necessity, be mindful of this. As a community activist in Rivers State, Lebon960 puts it,

Among the community people, there is the ingrained sense of ownership, some inherent sense of ownership, a belief and conviction that the resources found in their land belong to them. And when the central government enacts a law that

> says the natural resources belong to the state, that creates a crisis, tension within the community. . . . If there is some form of equitable distribution and sharing of the resources expropriated from their land, it would reduce the grievances and tempo of conflicts.[9]

As already stated, 90 percent of participants argue that the issue of deprivation in the Niger Delta has been a well-established fact. One participant's view that reflects the generality of opinions on human needs and relative deprivation is paraphrased here. Participant Oloko510 argues that the issue of deprivation is a well-known issue, and it comes from the fact that once the government discover oil and gas in your environment, on your land, you cease to be the owner of that land. That is deprivation of the highest order. And when they mine this oil and obtain all the moneys accruing to it, the landowners are not considered as stakeholders. And by the Nigerian constitution, government has the right to all the money that come from the mining of oil and gas and they reserve the decision as to where they should spend the money, what they should spend it on. The people are left to cater for their own needs.

Participants argue that poverty is still very prevalent in the Niger Delta. And that there should be no excuse why those who live in the Niger Delta should live in poverty. And talking about poverty is synonymous with talking about poverty of the worst order—it is poverty of the lowest order where individuals, families cannot cater for their children in terms of basic needs, school fees, and even quality meals, not to talk about the need for housing, and so forth.

> So, the people continue to perceive that the government has been negligent, hostile, and non-caring. Such perception triggers resentment and conflict that would continue until things change for the better.[10]

On the roles of political structures in the sustenance and resurgence of resource conflicts, I posed the following questions:

5. *Could you please discuss the role political structures play in the festering and resurgence of the Niger Delta conflicts?*
6. *What are the key aspects of Nigeria's political structures that you feel are critical to understanding and managing the Niger Delta conflicts?*

Of the thirty participants, nineteen, or 63.33 percent, view the operation of Nigeria's federalism as being contrary to the true spirit of a federation, that the country's political structure is skewed against the oil-producing communities in the Niger Delta because these are minority groups. The federal government controls the natural resources and those who own the land from which the oil and gas are produced are excluded from the benefits. The strands of the observations are along the lines that Nigeria is supposed to be operating a federal system of government whereby the federating units are supposed to control and manage their resources and pay taxes to the government at the center. But what is operational on the ground is the reverse. An all powerful federal government, at the powerful center, exclusively controls the natural resources, the mineral resources in Nigeria. With the very inhuman Land Use Act, which takes away the resources from the traditional owners and gives them to the federal government, Nigeria's political system, participants argue, is structured in such a way that it will always stimulate, will always trigger conflict because it is viewed as a clear departure from what true federalism is all about. So long as that structure which is not acceptable to oil-producing communities that see themselves as those who have been bankrolling the Nigerian economy, as long as they are unhappy, they would continue to demand change or some sort of restructuring to the current operating system. And they also emphasize that so long as there is such contestation, as long as there are such demands and agitations that receive passive responses or no responses, there is bound to be agitation for change. Political structure is seen as acting as a conflict stimulus, resource conflict stimulus.

In this section, I discuss interview questions about mobilization of conflict actors, relationship between transnational oil corporations, and oil-producing communities.

7. *Reflecting on decades of conflicts, how have nonviolent methods vs. violent methods of protest impacted relations between transnational oil corporations and oil producing communities?*
8. *In response to community agitations, how do you view the standard operating practice of the transnational oil corporations and the government of Nigeria?*

Adopting peaceful means of protest does not appear to have paid off. Besides the experience of the Ogoni people, which was alluded to earlier in this chapter, there are the experiences of the Umuchem community in Etche Local Government of Rivers State in 1990 and Imiringi community in Bayelsa State in 2012, which participants referenced. The Umuechem people began a peaceful protest against Shell, demanding employment opportunities and social amenities in October 1991. The people alleged that Shell Oil drilling operations have had serious effects on them being predominantly farmers. They alleged that their farmlands had been acquired and their crops damaged with little or no compensation. The citizens of Umuechem also alleged that the Otamiri River from which they fetch water for domestic uses and drinking is polluted by sleeks of crude oil and industrial waste that rendered water unfit for human consumption.

Before embarking on the demonstration, the organizers informed Shell of the purpose and nature of the peaceful protest. In response, Shell allegedly wrote to the government and specially requested for the notorious Police Mobile Force (popularly called Kill and Go) to be sent to "protect their staff and equipment."[11] The police raided the community commando-style and at the end of it all, 80 persons were killed, and 495 houses razed or severely damaged. The military governor of Rivers State at the time instituted a Commission of Inquiry into the Umuechem Massacre due to public outcry. The Commission released its official report in 1991.

The experience of the Imiringi community in Bayelsa is particularly instructive for this study. Participant Pastor Albert530, previously cited above, recounted in detail the community interaction with Shell Petroleum Development Company (SPDC). His story goes that every year during the past decade the community was awarded the Shell Community Peace Award. Award comes with no monetary value, just a plaque. The award is in recognition that the Imiringi community has been a welcoming and peaceful host to Shell Oil employees and facilities.

In 2016 Imiringi indigenes approached the management of Shell to inquire why the community has not benefited from the development projects that the company provides for other host communities. Shell officials responded that there was no reason to provide social programs when there was no threat to their operations from the Imiringi Community. In other words, projects are provided to those communities that use violence or threaten to use violence against the personnel and facilities of Shell as incentives to prevent disruption of their operations. Participant Pastor Albert530 says community leaders could not comprehend the logic of the oil company, which they interpret to be an invitation for youths to take laws into their own hands. On the other hand, community leaders reckon that they should be rewarded for peaceful behavior.

Relations between transnational oil companies operating in the Niger Delta and the oil-producing communities have been, to say the least, tensed and characterized by bad blood. As indicated earlier in this book, the oil companies are closer to the people while the government is located hundreds of miles away. The communities tend to expect the IOCs to assist in providing social amenities which should be the traditional responsibility of government. The mobilization of the Ogoni people by Saro-Wiwa during 1990–1995 expanded the understanding and horizon of the oil-producing communities to their rights and potential benefits. Overtime the local communities began to make demands on the IOCs. Some of the encounters between the people and the oil companies were peaceful while others have led to clashes and violence.

All thirty participants, or 100 percent, believe that the manner oil companies conduct themselves among the host communities constitute a major driver of tension and conflict. Let us examine some of the comments of participants on the relationship between oil companies and oil-producing communities in the Niger Delta. Participants call attention to the fact that most of their communities are still in their pristine nature devoid of basic modern amenities. And then the oil companies that operate within their communities pollute their environment even as they claim they do not benefit from the crude oil mined in their territory. They claim that local citizens drink from the river, from the polluted river, and that the situation was getting worse due to petroleum-related pollution, spills seriously polluted swarms, rivers, creeks, even up to the Atlantic Ocean. All the participants made references to the Bonga oil spills, major oil spills that occurred in December 2011 and many other spills and leaks in other locations throughout the Niger Delta.

The Bonga incident of December 2011 was a major oil spill and gas blow out on the Atlantic Ocean which occurred from Shell Oil facility. Three participants who were eyewitnesses said the fire lasted for almost two months without being put out and that three weeks after the spills at Bonga that there was another major gas blow out at the Chevron's oil and gas wellhead located in Kula Ama. Participants claim that the fire lasted for almost two months before it went off on its own and the sea was highly polluted to the point that large and small aquatic lives like whales, dolphins, and crayfish died. These are some of the experiences of inhabitants of oil-producing communities that fuel resentment. Participant Zima450 pinpoints what is considered a constant reminder of the harmful impact of oil companies:

> Gas is being continuously flared 24/7, wasting this finite resource. It is being burnt off daily and polluting the environment causing cancer and other ailments through our plants, through the water we drink, through the animals we eat, we get these carcinogenic and other elements that come from the petroleum industry.[12]

Another participant Prince730 on location in Imiringi, Yenegoa, allege that based on his personal experience, that the international oil companies (IOCs), most of the times, are good at breaking Memorandum of Understandings (MOUs) with the oil-producing communities and that they are not straightforward in their dealings. They go into MOUs with communities and at the end of the day, they break them. They do not want to honor the agreement or understanding they sign with host communities believing they could always intimidate the local people. One example provided was the MOU negotiated by Shell Nigeria and the people of Kolo Creek. In 2011, Shell had an MOU with Imiringi, Otosega, Elebele, and Oruma, four oil-producing communities in this area collectively called Kolo Creek. The agreement was that as long as there was power (light) in Shell's facility, in their camp, they would provide electricity to the four communities of Kolo Creek. Participant Prince730 aver that Shell did not live up to their word. After several years, the participant mobilized the people, youth, and women to confront Shell peacefully.

Participant alleged that Shell called the governor of Bayelsa State and that the government brought in a private security outfit called "Operation Fandangbe" and they, Operation Fandangbe raided their communities, and arrested a lot of youths, injured, and beat up women and chiefs.

A third participant, Belema980 says the profit-making multinational oil companies do not behave like good corporate citizens. Also speaking from personal experience in another Niger Delta oil-producing community participant Belema980 suggests that oil companies come into a community and take away the resources of the people in a very brazen, arrogant, and disrespectful manner and they cause social dislocations in the local communities because the oil companies' personnel are loaded with substantial cash, both local and local foreign cash. There have been stories of communities where oil workers coming into the communities take over the wives and girlfriends of some of the poor men in those communities. Those practices lead to resentment and frustration among the local people and adding to continuation of conflict.

The standard operating practice of the IOCs in response to community demands and grievances as identified by participants could be summarized thus:

Rather than negotiate with the host communities, the IOCs appeal to the federal authorities to send security forces to guard and protect them while they engage in oil production.

- The IOCS argue that it is not their responsibility to develop the local communities. They say this is the responsibility of the government.
- They, IOCs, argue that they pay taxes, royalties, and mining rents to the federal government and so therefore, they fulfill their obligation to the government and contribute to the growth and well-being of the country.
- The IOCs argue that the oil-producing communities should direct their petitions and demands to the government.
- Regarding the claims of the oil-producing communities that oil production cause environmental pollution through oil spills and gas flaring, the IOCs say that most oil spills are caused by sabotage. And when the communities take the IOCs to court to seek redress, the IOCs are in the habit of appealing court rulings rather than pay compensations, settle out of court, and/or negotiate with the host communities.

- In response to public demonstrations and protests, the IOCs usually request protection by soldiers and the Police Mobile Force, a security unit especially notorious for its brutality. This has, in practice, led to loss of lives and property and increased tension and bad blood between the IOCs and the host communities.[13]

A prominent environmental activist in Bayelsa recalled an encounter with a senior management personnel with Shell, during an intervention on behalf of the Biseni community. Participant Matata220 asserts that a Shell official said something to the effect that "If not for people like you (referencing a local environmental action group), helping them (the Biseni people) they would have been forgotten because they are bush people."[14] And this statement was credited to a senior management staff responsible for Community Relations for a major IOC operating in the area. This attitude, the participant claims, reflects the disdain which the IOCs has for the local oil-producing communities in which they operate.

The following section contains questions on perceptions of relevant actors on factors accounting for the lingering conflicts. The provision of options in question nine below emerged during the pilot research, a suggestion by participants.

9. *On a scale of "1-to-5," "1" being the most important and "5" being the least important, what aspects of governance, do you believe, are responsible for the perpetuation of the conflicts?*
10. *Please explain why you rank them so.* The responses of participants are tabulated in this section in ranking order:
    1. Poor or ineffective governance—bad government policies that negate the principles of federalism. Poor management of resources at all levels of government.
    2. The lack of a comprehensive government policy to address the complaints of the Niger Delta people. Absence of a comprehensive Niger Delta policy.
    3. Government neglect of the Niger Delta.
    4. Failure of government to listen to the people of the Niger Delta. No listening mechanism.

Participants explain their decisions to give the rankings as follows (see Table 5.2) Poor or ineffective governance is given as the main reason for the continuation of the Niger Delta conflicts. Poor or ineffective governance is the umbrella term for identified government policies that negatively impact the Niger Delta people and that are considered contrary to the principles of federalism and the mismanagement of resources at all levels of government.

Table 5.2 Aspects of Resource Governance as Ranked by Participants

Rank	*Aspects of Resource Governance*	*Number of Participants Ranking*	*Percentage (%)*
1	Poor or ineffective governance—bad government policies that negate the principles of federalism. Poor management of resources at all levels of government.	21	70
2	The lack of a comprehensive government policy to address the complaints of the Niger Delta people. Absence of a comprehensive Niger Delta policy.	18	60
3	Government neglect of the Niger Delta.	25	83
4	Failure of government to listen to the people of the Niger Delta. No listening mechanism.	20	67

Source: Data generated by the author.

These government policies include (a) Petroleum Decree of 1969, which allocates the ownership of oil and gas resources to the federal government of Nigeria and denies the right of the Niger Delta people to the crude oil and gas resources found in their territory; (b) the Land Use Decree of 1978, which gives the control of all lands in a state to the governor; and (c) the Revenue Allocation formula which spells out how all federally collected revenue are shared among the tiers of government—federal, state, and local governments. Changes would need to be made to these policies to address the grievances of the people of the Niger Delta and to work toward resolving the conflicts. The current revenue formula allocates 52.68 percent to the federal government, 26.72 percent to state governments, and 20.60 percent to local governments with a special 13 percent derivation to oil-producing states.

Participants ranked poor or ineffective governance high in helping to perpetuate the conflicts. This they attribute to the promotion of selfish interests by those in authority, lack of institutional capacity, and misappropriation of funds. Absence of a comprehensive Niger Delta policy on the part of the federal government means that the complaints of the people are unattended to. The Niger Delta has been neglected by successive Nigerian government since independence. Leaders of the regions have made this allegation for decades, as indicated in chapter 2. Most participants, twenty-two out of thirty, or 73 percent, say government and the IOCs do not listen to the complaints of the people. Participants suggest that given the structure of Nigeria, the fact that some groups are very dominant in terms of numbers, in terms of population, in terms of political power happened to be those that are not bearing the brunt of extraction of mineral resources, they seem to pay deaf ears to what is going on, to the cries of the people of the Niger Delta. And so as far as they (the dominant groups) are concerned, the status quo should be maintained.

Some participants suggest that rather than listen to the people; the government has two standard approaches or responses—the use of state violence and co-optation. These participants point to alleged use of heavy state violence by the Nigerian government to intimidate and suppress the agitation of Niger Delta people which they claim has been documented by independent groups like Amnesty International, Human Rights Watch, and CLO. In discussing these observations Participant Lebon960 says Nigeria had been run by military governments for decades and that the military demonstrate disrespect for human lives, disrespect for human rights, disrespect for anything and are quick to engage violence and other intimidating tactics in any confrontations, a kind of military mentality. Thus, if the communities attempt to raise an issue, they would be crushed or co-opted. Participants say the reason conflict lingers in the Niger Delta is that issues that would lead to resolution are not addressed.

This section discusses suggestions and recommendations about managing the conflicts.

11. *In order of importance, what are your suggestions for managing the Niger Delta conflicts?*

While most of the participants, twenty-eight out of thirty, or 93.33 percent, made suggestions, I believe it is appropriate to use quote from one participant that generally reflect the key points of all the respondents who discussed this question. Participant Zima450 proposes the following,

> Government need to put up a new framework to include all actors and stakeholders to brainstorm in a conducive environment on the conflicts. The process and the discussion should not be skewed to the advantage of any particular actors or stakeholders. This proposed framework must be all-encompassing, inclusive, participatory, just, and sustainable. The framework should be designed around the actors and the multifaceted dimensions of resource conflicts in the Niger Delta. It is only when all actors and stakeholders bring their issues and interests to the table, to consider their merits, could a formidable framework be negotiated.[15]

Participants also suggest that the federal structure exists by name but in actual operation it is unitary in character, like a unitary state and that it was important and critical for Nigeria's political system be restructured to reflect a federalist structure that guarantees more community rights. They suggest that government should adopt true federalism, run Nigeria as an authentic federation where the federating units control their resources and pay taxes to the government at the center. Arguing that the people of the Niger Delta desire good governance, participants suggest that the federal government must be seen to be working to improve the lives of all citizens, especially those of the Niger Delta. Government should be transparent and accountable to the people.

12. *What are your recommendations for managing resource conflicts in the Niger Delta region?*

The participants made several recommendations for managing the protracted conflicts in the Niger Delta based on their personal experiences. Table 5.3 reflects the recommendations made.

13. *Any additional comments that you would like to make about the topic that you feel is important for me to note?*

Only eight out of the thirty participants, or 26 percent, made additional comments in this section. The remainder, most of the participants, chose not to provide additional comments. The comments targeted three areas: (a) that IOCs be made to adopt international best practices to prevent environmental pollution in the oil-producing communities, (b) resources derived from the Niger Delta be used to develop the area, and (c) the responsibility for resolving the Niger Delta conflict falls to the Nigerian government. The following comment by participant Ibinabo220 is representative:

> So, the root causes of the conflict are environmental degradation, lack of social amenities, and then our being excluded from the benefits of the natural resources that belong to us both in the management and utilization. I would say the onus to resolve the conflict is on the government and the oil companies. I believe that the government listens to the oil companies more than the citizens. We do not want oil companies to operate with double standards. They should operate here the same way they operate in the Netherlands or America.[16]

A common theme that emerges from this study includes the perception that resource governance has the most significant impact on the continuity, elongation, and sporadic outbursts of conflict in Nigeria's Niger Delta. Most of the respondents, twenty-nine of the thirty participants, or 96 percent, suggest that resource governance account for the persistence of the Niger Delta conflicts. This view is tied to the realization that Nigeria's economy is bankrolled

Table 5.3 Recommendations for Managing Conflict

	Recommendations for Managing Conflict	Number of Participants Who Made Suggestions	Percentage (%)
1.	The government must take the initiative to bring all parties to the conflict together, to open up the space for genuine, constructive dialogue.	30	100
2.	The government must demonstrate sincerity and transparency in its dealings with the Niger Delta.	26	86
3.	There should be continuity of government policy and programs designed to respond to the demands of the Niger Delta.	22	73
4.	Government should address the issue of ownership of oil and gas resources. The oil-producing communities from which natural resources are derived should also be beneficiaries as a matter of policy.	30	100
5.	Government should ensure equitable distribution of revenues in such a way that the derivation principle is upheld.	28	93
6.	Government should stop the use of state violence to suppress the demands of Niger Delta people. Government should engage in dialogue instead.	30	100
7.	Government should urgently take measures to mitigate environmental damage caused by oil production.	29	96
8.	Victims of state violence, human rights violations, and crude oil exploitation in the Niger Delta should be appropriately compensated.	27	90

Source: Data generated by the author.

mainly by oil and gas resources found in the Niger Delta. The Niger Delta people believe that the way the oil and gas resources are managed has disproportionately deprived them of access and benefits of the natural resources found in their natural environment. Below is a sample of the comments of the participants. A participant, a lecturer at the University of Education, Port Harcourt, River State, participant Dogo820, says resource governance is at the center of the entire Niger Delta conflicts. Governance is at the fulcrum, is at the center; it is at the middle of the entire conflicts in the Niger Delta regarding oil exploration. In answering the question, "how is resource governance at the center of resource conflicts in the Niger Delta?" participant Dogo820 says,

> Think of governance in terms of, we have natural resources, crude oil, and gas here in this region. Now, who are those who control and administer these resources? Do the Niger Delta people control and administer these resources? No, they do not! That is the anger of the people.[17]

Another participant, a female, one of six female respondents, a peace advocate in Bayelsa, participant PeaceLady950 has the following comments:

> The major cause of conflicts in the Niger Delta has been centered on resource ownership, management, and extraction issues around them. We have had situations where communities that are relatively peaceful but once crude oil is found, and extraction activities begin we found out that the reverse is now the case.[18]

A second theme pertains to the belief that the issue of ownership, control, and distribution of natural resources would need to be addressed to begin the process toward resolving the Niger Delta conflicts. This has been a major push by advocates of reform of Nigeria's federalism from the Niger Delta, commonly called "resource control." A majority of respondents, twenty-one out of thirty, or 70 percent of participants, propose that there is an innate conviction among the citizens in this region that crude oil and gas resources belong to them, that they say, "we own the resources." All other demands or grievances seem to originate from this point of view. A well-known community leader participant Amba230 offers the following perspective—among the community people, there is an ingrained sense of ownership, some inherent sense of ownership, a belief and conviction that the resources found in their land belong to them. Whether they are within or beyond reach, whether it means that the resources are several miles deep in the ground or not, the common assumption is that these resources, be they mineral resources, or water resources, they belong to the people. Or even anything above the earth growing up. It is assumed that these natural resources are within their territory. And when any national government enact a law declaring that the government are the owners of the natural resources found in the environment of the communities in the Niger Delta, and that whether government pay compensation to communities or not, that it is the law of the land. Such a position is a clear invitation to conflict.

Another participant, Erebo470, a women leader and teacher, echoes the aforementioned viewpoint, that the government policy that declares that the crude oil found in the Niger Delta belongs to the federal government is clearly contrary, is in direct negation of the traditional belief, the cultural practice of the people for generations. The belief system in the region gives the right of ownership of land to a family, group of families, or lineage and that one inherits from one's parents. She argues that government policy that usurps the right to the property on their land, in this case, crude oil, does not sit well with the people of the region, suggesting that this was the first point of conflict between the federal government and the Niger Delta people. This is a core source of the Niger Delta conflict given that Nigerian policy grants the ownership and control of crude oil and gas to the federal government, according to Opuko870:

> In terms of equitable distribution of resources in our territory, the perception of the community people is that the resources, are ours, "we own the resources," and that any government or any group of persons who come to challenge our right, you are constituting a threat to our ownership and that is the first point of conflict.[19]

Still on ownership, most participants draw attention to the Petroleum Industry Bill (PIB) which was later renamed Petroleum Industry Governance Bill (PIGB) that has stagnated in the National Assembly for a decade and has not been passed. The bill had proposed that oil-producing communities in the Niger Delta acquire 10 percent equity shares in the oil companies operating in their territory. Participants lament that the hopes of the oil-producing communities have since been dashed given that the oil companies and other special interest groups have fought tooth and nail to prevent the bill to see the light of day.

A third theme is the perception that the contribution the Niger Delta region has made and continues to make to Nigeria is not acknowledged and compensated by the Nigerian state. Twenty-one out of thirty or 70 percent of interviewees hold the perception that the Niger Delta people are not accorded proper recognition and compensation, given their economic contributions to the stability of the Nigerian state. A participant, a director of community resource center, participant Pado690 argues that given the structure of Nigeria, the fact that some groups are very dominant over the others and incidentally those who are dominant in terms of numbers, in terms of population, in terms of political power happened to be those that are not bearing the brunt of extraction of mineral resources, they seem to pay deaf ears to what is going on, to the cries of the people of the Niger Delta.

Connecting this to my literature review, it is instructive to note that a well-known Nigerian commentator, Cyril Obi (2012) argues this point too. Obi writes:

> Although an object of, and fuel for volatile politics and conflict, oil remains the glue holding Nigeria—a multi-ethnic social formation and Africa's putative hegemonic power-together in a complex but rather fractious unity. (Obi, 2012, 24)

Leaders and activists in the region, for example, claim that they are excluded or marginalized in federal appointments, allocation of oil mining licenses, award of oil-related contracts, employment opportunities, and award of scholarships. Chairman of CLO and community traditional ruler, participant Nanga588, also the Chairman of CLO, Bayelsa State Branch proposes that the new policy on modular refineries would not work. The refineries were meant to prevent further environmental damage; however, participant Nanga588 argues that the fifty-nine licenses issued by the Nigerian government in 2017 went to companies and individuals outside of the Niger Delta region. Participants say that practices such as this continue to fuel the perception of marginalization of the Niger Delta people in the scheme of things in Nigeria. Without the participation, the input of the people of the Niger Delta, none of the policies or programs of the government would work, the participants say. They also contend that the idea of modular refineries was proposed at the height of the operations of the NDA, in an attempt to get the militants off the creeks and to bring them to the negotiating table and to divert attention from the fighting. It has been three years since the Avengers agreed to negotiate with the government and nothing has been done. The rights activist also contend that the UNEP clean-up of Ogoni land has yet to take off after six years and wonders why talk about modular refineries when the UNEP clean-up in Ogoni has not taken off.

The fourth recurrent theme found in my study is a parallel feeling of dispossession and the genuineness of the demands of the people of the Niger Delta. A sense of being cheated that they do not matter in the scheme of things, side by side with perception of being persecuted, because they are minority groups, and lacking political influence. A traditional ruler, participant Chief Nelson101 from the region, described the people of the Niger Delta as "a dispossessed people." Echoing this sentiment is a regional director of a grassroots community environmental group based in Bayelsa, participant Golam250 argues that

> Military decrees like the petroleum act and the land use decree of 1978 were used by military governments in Nigeria to expropriate, to take away ownership from the rightful owners of the resources. And so, these are some of the constitutional or legal instruments through which ownership is denied our people. This practice is widespread in the oil industry where government officials will remain in Abuja and give license to some persons to come to explore and exploit crude oil in the Niger Delta, without even the people that own the land being

part of the agreement. You are surprised, one day you see people entering your forest, your bush. And that has been a source of worry to our people.[20]

There is a resonance with the claim about a lack of development in the region and the feeling of relative deprivation. The sheer lack of basic social amenities like clean pipe-borne water, health facilities, electricity, and decent housing in the oil-producing communities in juxtaposition with those made available to employees of the IOCs is a source of grievance. Dokpesi and Ibiezugbe (2012, 64) capture this sentiment in the following words:

> The underdevelopment of the region has partly been attributed to its difficult physical terrain. Ironically, the oil companies create worker settlements, equipped with modern facilities such as electricity, water, housing, telecommunications, and recreation, within installations in an effort to create comfort for their employees. This sharply contrasts with the death and decay witnessed in host communities that adjoin these oil companies' facilities. This unequal access to modern infrastructure and social services within the same environment, coupled with neglect by the past governments, has attracted resentment from members of these oil-bearing communities.

A prominent community leader in Offoin-Ama community, in the Kula Kingdom, Akuku-Toru Local Government of Rivers State participant Kula740, bemoaned the neglect, hardship, and poverty in the community, and lamented that SPDC has not provided basic infrastructure:

> SPDC has operated here for 40 years and there is nothing to show for it. We lack basic amenities. We do not have portable water, no good school, no good health facilities. Life is practically unbearable in this environment. We know the hazards associated with oil and gas operation; the benzene components of crude oil, the mercury it produces, and all other chemicals associated with oil and gas exploration. Our community also hosts a gas injection plant and its booster stations. Offoin-Ama hosts the "6 & 8" pipeline, delivery link, eastern gathering line, and Trans Niger Delta/Nembe trunk pipeline. (Sukubo, 2018)

The fifth common theme suggests that IOCs appear to exert some degree of influence over the government of Nigeria and able to lobby against potential unfavorable government policies. This is because the IOCs seem to have undue influence on the government regardless of the government in power, given the financial contributions of the oil industry to Nigeria's economy. Participants point to the inability of government to compel the IOCs to obey the laws governing the oil industry. Seventeen participants out of thirty, or 56 percent, share this view. For instance, since 1992 government has enacted legislations prohibiting gas flaring, but the IOCs flout these laws without consequences. Explicating this point, the NGO expert, participant Alale310, asserts that

> The transnational oil and gas corporations are operating in a lawless environment and they have taken advantage of that. The Nigerian government runs a mono-product economy. They depend heavily on crude oil. And you have a very parasitic and lazy ruling class. They do not think of doing any other thing apart from the petrodollars. You have this kind of situation where the Nigerian elite are all dependent on the oil companies. The oil companies dictate almost everything. We do not have any initiative. They run our intelligence services. They run our so-called community development projects. They run almost everything. These things are not done in the open, but some of us, we know. These are some of the issues, and some of the contradictions in Nigeria, with our overdependence on oil.[21]

These views are critical for my research especially because they connect the experiences of the Niger Delta, the focus of my study, to the literature. Azar's PSC theory, its fourth step, discusses external linkages, references to the role of corporations linking local economies and communities to the international market, creating distortions. It also discusses how the response of such a state to conflict is directly tied to the impact of the corporations. In the Niger Delta, the IOCs as we have seen by the comments of the participants, by their economic influence, capital base, technological skills, industrial output, and political leverage are so powerful they tend to prevail in interactions and confrontations with the local or the national authorities and/or communities.

The final common theme is environmental pollution caused by oil exploration and production that affect the agricultural land and rivers and threaten the occupations and livelihood of the people in the oil-producing communities. Incidents of oil spills, gas flares, and other ecological threats like acid rain pollute farmlands, rivers, and rainfall which in turn contaminate underground water sources. Eighty percent of participants, or twenty-four out of thirty, say they are concerned about the threat posed to the Niger Delta environment by oil production. Participant Zima450's comments are germane to this view:

> The demands of the people of the Niger Delta and the local communities are genuine. They are just and are embedded in the fabrics of their lives. And the demands will be sustained over time. It is not something any form of suppression can eliminate. We are talking about a people whose livelihood have been eroded by industrial exploitation of the natural resources in the region. So, they are left with hunger, they are left with degraded environment, they are left

> with infertile farmlands, and polluted creeks. The question is, how would they survive? So, for them to be able to survive, they would continue to agitate for the restoration of their environment. They would continue to agitate for best practices in resource extraction in the region in order to safeguard the dependent ecosystems. It's about the lives of the people in the region.[22]

The government and the IOCs have not shown any zeal to introduce measures to protect the environment, prevent incidents of pollution, and remedy occurrences. The few instances where laws do exist, there have been a lack of monitoring and enforcement. One significant case mentioned is the UNEP report on Ogoni. In 2011, the UNEP released a report alleging severe ecological damage caused by oil exploration and called for the government and Shell Oil to immediately implement mitigation measures to clean up the environmental damage to the community. No significant progress has been made by the government to implement the recommendations of the report.

An uncommon theme is that government has a conflict of interest, being a partner with the IOCs operating in Nigeria, and thus unlikely to be a fair arbiter in the conflict with the Niger Delta people. Therefore, the argument goes that the conflicts have lingered primarily because the government has consistently sided with a key actor or group of actors, the IOCs operating in the region against its own citizens, the oil-bearing communities.

A contradictory theme emerges regarding the perspective of those who are in favor of the adoption of violent methods of agitation and those who support or advocate utilizing peaceful methods of struggle. There seems to be almost an even divide between the two groups as fourteen out of thirty of the participants, or 46.67 percent, were in support of the use of violent methods to attain the goals of the Niger Delta struggle, while sixteen out of thirty participants, or 53.33 percent, expressed their preference for the use of nonviolent methods of struggle to accomplish the aspirations of the people of the Niger Delta. A question might arise about if the presidency of Jonathan contributed to this contradiction given that my interviews were conducted after the Jonathan presidency, indeed during the Buhari presidency, could this have colored the answers? I do not believe that conducting the interviews after the Jonathan presidency colored the answers by the participants. Here is why. The methods of struggle under consideration (peaceful or violent methods) predated the Jonathan presidency and continued, although in differing scales, during the reigns of both the Jonathan and Buhari administrations.

Those who advocate violence or support the use of violent agitation to advance the cause of the Niger Delta argue that so long as the crude oil is flowing, providing the needed revenue to maintain its basic obligations, that the Nigerian state, no matter the government in power, would not address the demands of the people of the Niger Delta. And that the only language the

Nigerian government understands was violence or threat of violence. Those who hold this view allude to two decades of struggle and the violent manner the government had repressed the struggle. They argue that if the government were serious about resolving the issues at stake, it would have engaged the communities and begun some remedies or mitigation measures. Participants draw attention to the use of mobile policemen and soldiers to quell protests in oil-producing communities in Umuechem in Etche and several communities in Ogoni in 1990 and 1994/1995 respectively.

On the other hand, those who believe in peaceful advocacy, as indicated earlier, 53.33 percent of participants, aver that the nonviolent approach still offers hope for the people of the region. They point to the loss of lives and property, the disruption of social life, and the permanent deployment of soldiers and other security agents in the community by the government as they repress the demands of the people and counter the activities of militants. Participant PeaceLady950 appears to reflect the perspective of this group:

> Nonviolence has been the best approach so far. It might be slow, right? Why people run away from it is because it is slow. It is slow because you really cannot get the desired results as soon as you want it. But they say, slow and steady, you win the race. As you go slow and steady making your points heard and making your voices heard, you will be recognized and someday, even if it is not done, people will make reference, to say, this should have been the best option. So, I think nonviolence has always been the best.[23]

One participant, Pastor Albert530, a prince, stated that though he would not bear arms, that he supported those who chose to do so, because, according this participant, a son of a community chief, the government bears the responsibility given their refusal to engage and work with those who advocate reforms peacefully and nonviolent manner.

I have discussed in this chapter the perceptions and grievances of the people of the Niger Delta, the common themes in my research, utilizing information derived from databases, analysis of the NIIA collection on the Niger Delta conflicts, and semi-structured one-to-one interviews I conducted in Nigeria. Resource governance is both at the heart of the conflicts in the Niger Delta and the ideal place to seek solutions. Most participants in my study identified resource governance, the policies that spell out the process of managing the crude oil and gas resources that sustain the Nigerian economy, as the fulcrum, the key issue impacting conflicts in the Niger[24] Delta. The calls for restructuring Nigeria's federal system are basically due to the dissatisfaction of the way the revenue derived from crude oil is managed and shared. I also discussed the changes in the identities and influence of the actors and stakeholders, that emergent actors and networks in the conflicts are very youthful and violent, and operate underground, and that some engage in bunkering. Issues identified for being responsible for the perpetuation of the conflicts and the suggestions for resolving the conflicts were also discussed. In chapter 6, I discuss the heart of the matter, the ideal place to seek solutions.

NOTES

1. Interviewees voluntarily gave oral consent to use their responses and words and I utilize codes and pseudonyms to protect the identities of respondents and participants.
2. Personal interview, Port Harcourt, Rivers State, Nigeria, November 2017.
3. Personal interview, Botem Tai, Rivers State, Nigeria, December 2017.
4. Personal interview, Port Harcourt, Rivers State, Nigeria, November 2017.
5. Personal interview, Port Harcourt, Rivers State, Nigeria, December 2017.
6. Personal interview, Port Harcourt, Rivers State, Nigeria, November 2017.
7. Personal interview, Bodo, Rivers State, Rivers State, December 2017.
8. Personal interview, Port Harcourt, Rivers State, Nigeria, November 2017.
9. Personal interview, Bodo, Rivers State, Nigeria, November 2017.
10. Personal interview, Port Harcourt, Rivers State, Nigeria, December 2017.
11. See a copy of the Shell letter in the appendix of the official Commission of Inquiry Report, 1991.
12. Personal interview, Amasoma, Bayelsa State, Nigeria, December 2017.
13. See the websites of Shell Oil (www. shellnigeria.com.ng) and Chevron (www. chevron/worldwide/nigeria) for more of the claims of the oil giants. Shell has sections devoted to Ogoniland.
14. Personal interview, Amasoma, Bayelsa State, Nigeria, December 2017.
15. Personal interview, Port Harcourt, Rivers State, Nigeria, November 2017.
16. Personal interview, Imiringi, Bayelsa State, December 2017.
17. Personal interview, Port Harcourt, Rivers State, Nigeria, December 2017.
18. Personal interview, Yenegoa, Bayelsa, State, Nigeria, November 2017.
19. Personal interview, Bodo, Rivers State, Nigeria, November 2017.
20. Personal interview, Yenogoa, Bayelsa State, Nigeria, December 2017.
21. Personal interview, Port Harcourt, Rivers State, Nigeria, November 2017.
22. Personal interview, Port Harcourt, Rivers State, Nigeria, November 2017.
23. Personal interview, Yenogoa, Bayelsa State, Nigeria, December 2017.
24. Personal interviews, Bayelsa & Rivers States, Nigeria, Nov-Dec. 2017.

Chapter 6

The Heart of the Matter

The Ideal Place to Seek Solutions

Substantive changes have occurred during two decades of conflict in the Niger Delta including among the main actors, stakeholders and networks, the roles political structures play, and the experiences of the communities in interaction with IOCs and the government. In this section, I discuss the key findings of my study and the issues to address to find solutions and mitigation by structuring the results using the following subheadings:

IDENTITIES AND AGENDAS OF STAKEHOLDERS AND NETWORKS IN THE NIGER DELTA CONFLICTS

To have a deeper understanding of the persistent conflicts requires a closer look at the identities of actors, stakeholders, and the agendas that propel them. Participants in this study identify three critical layers of actors in the conflicts in the Niger Delta conflicts—the government, the international oil companies, and the oil-producing communities. These actors are considered the primary actors. So, therefore, to be specific, the primary actors and stakeholders are the federal government of Nigeria with capital in Abuja, IOCs like Shell, MobilChevron, Agip, Total, and Panocean, and the oil-producing communities. SPDC is the leading transnational oil exploration company responsible for 60 percent of total oil and gas production in the country. In Ogoni land in Rivers State, for example, SPDC has six oil fields, ninety-six oil wells, and five flow stations at Bomu, Bodo West, Ebubu, Korokoro, and Yorla. The oil-producing communities are hosts to the IOCs, they voluntarily or coercively let their farmland, rivers, and creeks to be used as campsites, drilling sites, tank farms, flow lines, flow stations, oil fields, oil wells, and depots. The presence of the IOCs, their employees, and facilities have significant impacts on the livelihood of local population of these communities. Besides the more visible environmental pollution, there are also social and economic dislocations and disruptions to the ways of life of the people. Other subsidiary stakeholders mentioned include oil marketers, oil servicing companies, holders of oil lifting licenses, security agencies that protect the oil companies and their facilities, and community groups like CBOs and CSOs. The subsidiary actors are further subdivided into community networks and business networks.

Community networks include traditional rulers, women's groups, youth groups, and families and lineages. In some of the youth groups, there are cult groups, gangs, and militants; some are unarmed while others are peaceful. One participant who wears many hats—a son of a traditional ruler, a pastor, and community activist—suggests that families within host communities must be considered as key actors, for according to this participant, land ownership belongs to families, groups of families, and lineages. Obviously, this view is inconsistent with the Land Use Decree of 1978, which vests control of land in the governor of a state. In my view, this is a clash of traditional beliefs and the superimposition of the neocolonial state over vestiges of precolonial structures. And where crude oil is not discovered, local villages still have to exercise ownership except in case where the piece of land is earmarked for a road or any government project. Business networks include oil lifting licensees, oil marketers, contractors, agents, trade unions, oil servicing groups, and transportation companies.

Nigeria Watch, a research database that monitors lethal violence, conflicts, and human security in Nigeria's Niger Delta since 2006, identifies Shell, ChevronTexaco, ExxonMobil, Total, Ent Nazionale Idrocarburi, ConocoPhillips, and the NNPC as the major oil companies, major stakeholders in the conflicts (nigeriawatch.org).

Significant changes have occurred among the identities and influence of key actors and networks in the Niger Delta conflicts. While the traditional actors and stakeholders such as the federal government, the IOCs, and host communities remain key players in the Niger Delta conflicts, the most changes have been noticed in the identities, agenda, and influences of the youth, community agitators, and informal networks of economic actors on the ground. The most significant changes are seen among the protagonists and advocates of reforms in the Niger Delta. The main activists on the ground consists mainly of youthful elements, including women, who chose to bear arms and adopt a violent approach to achieve their goals.

Contrary to the early days of struggle in early 1990–1995, when the leading advocates were mature, middle-aged men and women like Saro-Wiwa, who adopted nonviolent and peaceful methods of struggle and operated publicly, the current advocates are mostly much younger men and women in their teens and twenties, and they operate underground and chose to bear arms in the struggle. They form themselves into heavily armed and fortified insurrection groups and engage the security forces, targeting oil company workers and oil industry infrastructure. They kidnap oil workers for a ransom and blow up oil pipelines and installations.

One participant, Prof. Olule840, in comparing the actors of the early days of the conflict to the current actors, infers that the new actors are more aggressive, their style and system of struggle is different from what the Ogoni people did. This participant claims that (a) the Ogoni people never engaged in destroying pipelines; (b) The Ogoni people never engaged in killing foreigners and also never engaged in kidnapping and ransoming oil workers; and (c) That the Ogoni people were nonviolent in their approach. They were carrying green branches, and demonstrating peacefully, and asking for what belongs to them. The Ogoni people were using the pen, and through writing and presenting the issues before the international community. In comparison, participant Prof. Oule840 argues that now the style of the struggle is taking matters into your hands.

> Taking matters into your hands, takes different forms. It involves outright violence, seizing of human beings, killing, and all that. So, the identities of the actors have changed, the style, strategy, the networks, and the methods of struggle have changed.[1]

There has been a proliferation of these groups that chose to bear arms for the struggle, popularly called militants. The militants have their camps in the thick mangrove forests in the mouth of the delta. They boast of their own hierarchy and their top commanders bear names like General Africa, General Boyloaf, General Bin Ladin, General Jamabo, General Joshua McIver, GOC Tompolo, General Ateke Tom, General Ogunbus, and General Torunawe. Some of them negotiated with the government and took advantage of the government's amnesty program that promised no prosecution for the militants who submit their weapons and recant armed struggle. As an offshoot of the amnesty, some of the top hierarchy were hired as security consultants to the federal government assisting to contain oil theft and provide general intelligence to the government. This process of appeasement and co-optation has pitted some groups against one another leading to continued breakaway groups and further proliferation of more militant groups with divergent agenda.

Some other informal actors also emerged and engage in bunkering, a common name for oil theft. Crude oil is siphoned from pipelines and sold in the international oil market. These groups that engage in bunkering are motivated by economic gains and, also, because they claim they could not find employment opportunities. These informal groups and actors have indeed had significant impact on the Nigeria economy. The Nigeria Minister of State for Petroleum Resources announced in February 2017 that the country lost $100 billion in oil revenue in 2016 due to attacks by militants in the Niger Delta and that oil production fell by as much as one million barrels a day in the same year. The emergence of these informal groups and their influence in the Niger Delta resonate with a perspective in the literature of resource governance which proposes that:

> Resources did not extract and sell themselves; it is done by particular actors. Analysts therefore need to understand the identities of those actors, how they operated and crucially, what political relationships and agendas influenced them. (Williams, 2011, 77–78)

From the above, I can conclude that my finding agrees with the literature. In summary, the three critical sets of actors and stakeholders in the Niger Delta are Nigeria's federal government, the international oil companies, and the oil-producing communities. The oil-producing communities are made up of chiefs, traditional rulers, and leaders of community development committees, and other CBOs. There are also the state governments of oil-producing states and local government councils. Other subsidiary stakeholders include oil marketers, oil servicing companies, holders of oil lifting licenses, security agencies that protect the oil companies and their facilities. The most significant changes in the identity and influence of the community actors, however, are seen among the youthfulness of most stakeholders. The actors are younger, including youth from several other ethnic groups in the Niger Delta, beyond the Ogoni who started the struggle; they operate underground, are now armed, and adopt violent means as opposed to the peaceful agitation of the early days, and engage in money-making ventures like operating refineries and kidnapping of oil workers.

PERCEPTION OF RELATIVE DEPRIVATION OF HUMAN NEEDS AND THE PERSISTENCE OF CONFLICTS

The lack of development, the absence of basic amenities or social services in the Niger Delta, particularly within the oil-bearing communities, continue to be a poster boy for the manifestation of the neglect of the Niger Delta. As indicated in chapter 2, the complaint of neglect and deprivation by the people of the Nigeria started before Nigeria's independence. I also discuss in chapter 2 the protestations of the leaders of the region to the British colonial authorities and their response in setting up the Willink Commission of Inquiry into the Fears of Minorities in 1958.

There are three perspectives to the perception on absence of social amenities contributing to the persistence of conflicts in the Niger Delta. First, is the perception that there is backwardness and lack of development in the region in comparison to other parts of Nigeria that do not produce crude oil. The feeling is that the oil resources of the Niger Delta have been used and continue to be used to develop other cities and regions in Nigeria while they, the communities in the Niger Delta, lack the basic social services like pipe-borne running water, electricity, healthcare facilities, and good schools. This stems from the awareness that the budgets of the three tiers of government—federal, state, and local governments—are mostly funded from the proceeds of crude oil and gas production.

I reproduce below a shortened version of the report by the Nigerian Extractive Industries Transparent Initiative (NEITI) 2015 due to its relevance. Oil and gas dominate the extractive sector in Nigeria, and the country holds 29 percent of Africa's proven oil reserves.

Most of the oil and gas activities are found in the Niger Delta in the southern part of the country. Nigeria is richly endowed with various types of mineral resources. Presently, there are over thirty-four mineral finds in commercial quantity spread across the entire country. Some key mineral resources include gold, coal, bitumen, iron ore, tantalite/columbite, lead/zinc sulfides, barytes, cassiterite, gemstones, talc, feldspar, and marble. Over 90 percent of the revenue accrued to the government in terms of royalties and other fees on minerals comes from quarrying operations according to the 2015 Solid Minerals Audit (Nigeria Extractive Industries Transparency Initiative, 2017).

Nigeria's oil and gas sector represents about 53 percent of government revenues. The total revenue flow to the Federation, other tiers of government and sub-national entities from all sources (including crude oil sales, taxes, royalties, and other incomes) came to $24.791billion. The total revenue from the 2015 Oil and Gas Industry Audit was $3,780,204,290 and while the total losses came to $2,267,426,012. The revenues reported by the government from the solid minerals sector in 2015 amounted to N69.2billion. Source: NEITI: Solid Minerals Sector Generated N69.2bn in 2015 (NEITI, 2017).

Second, there is the perception that while the oil-producing communities in the Nigeria's Niger Delta lack the basic social services, the campsites or location sites of the oil companies exploiting crude oil and gas in the area have all the comfort of those social amenities. This is a source of discontent. The surrounding communities live in darkness, without electricity and clean pipe-born water and other basic services, while the living quarters and offices of the oil companies have social services comparable to what obtains in Lagos, and other cities in the United States or the western world.

Third, there is the general perception of marginalization. The reason that the oil communities are neglected is that they are minorities and have no political leverage in the scheme of things in Nigeria. I must emphasize that these are perceptions of the people and these perceptions are deep-seated, and the people have held them for a long time. The perceptions are being reinforced by the perceived continued lack of targeted government response to redress the situation.

One of the main themes that emerge from the data as discussed in chapter 5 is the perception that in spite of the huge revenue the government derives from the oil and gas resources in the Niger Delta the region still wallows in poverty and the absence of basic social services. Twenty-seven out of thirty participants or 90 percent subscribe to this view. Twenty-five out of thirty participants, or 83.33 percent, suggest that government neglect and lack of development contribute to the perpetuation of the conflicts in the Niger Delta. Here, I reproduce what a prominent community leader in Offoin-Ama community, in the Kula Kingdom, Akuku-Toru LGA of Rivers State, participant Kula740, says about the condition of his community:

> SPDC has operated here for 40 years and there is nothing to show for it. We lack basic amenities. We do not have portable water, no good school, no good health facilities. Life is practically unbearable in this environment. (Sukubo, 2018)

A 2009 national survey conducted by Research and Marketing Services, an affiliate of Gallup International, and published by a Nigerian newspaper, *The Nation*, validated these claims. The report validated the "widespread belief that the lack of essential amenities and employment for Ogoni and Ijaw youths amounted to neglect, injustice, and a slant on the goose that lays the golden egg" (Oladesu, 2009, 13). According to the report, over 2,011 respondents from seven states, one each from the six political zones in Nigeria, plus Abuja, the federal capital territory, participated in the survey. Fifty-three percent of the respondents believed that the Niger Delta has been marginalized while 39 percent said the absence of infrastructural facilities was a major source of conflict and called for the provision of infrastructural facilities such as hospitals, tertiary institution, electricity, and water to the region. Thirty-seven percent of the respondents believed that youth unemployment was a key source of conflict in the region and advised the government to provide work for the local youth in the Niger Delta.

The Nigeria Watch database that I discuss in chapter 5 also cited lack of basic social amenities and lack of employment opportunities as issues that caused indigenes to frequently engage in public protests against the IOCs operating in their villages. In most cases, protesters like the women of Gbaramatu and Warri clans in Warri South West Local Government Area (LGA) in Delta State and people of Umuechem in the Etche LGA of Rivers

State, discussed in chapter 5, usually mention lack of social amenities, unemployment, and pollution as key grievances.

Similarly, the NIIA research collection on the Niger Delta discussed in chapter 5 listed absence of social amenities (5.83 percent) and lack of development/government, and IOC neglect (5.20 percent) as among the most frequent topics discussed about the Niger Delta conflict.

In addition, resource governance literature identifies failure of government to provide basic social amenities as one of three sources of feud:

> The local population accuses the federal government of three things: the passing of laws the population considers obnoxious, especially the Land Use Decree and the Terminal Tax; the forceful repression of protests the local population considers legitimate; and the refusal of government to produce basic amenities for the population. (Alao, 2007, 193)

In summary, a dominant theme that emerged from the data in this study is the widespread perception among the people in the Niger Delta that the failure of government to provide basic social amenities like electricity, clean pipe-borne water, healthcare services, and well-equipped schools to the communities is a source of anger, discontent, and helps to perpetuate conflicts. The realization that crude oil resources from the region has helped build major cities and provided comfort, opportunities, social infrastructure to other non-producing regions triggers anger and bitterness among the people. As indicated in chapter 5, several host communities have carried out several protests concerning non-provision of basic amenities by IOCs operating in their communities.

In this section I have shown some of the avenues through which the perception of relative deprivation of human needs, contributing to the persistence of conflict in the Niger Delta, is manifested in the dominant themes in the data, community protests, comments of participants, a published Gallup survey, the NIIA research collection, and consulted literature on the Niger Delta conflict.

THE ROLES NIGERIA'S POLITICAL STRUCTURES PLAY IN THE EMERGENCE, SUSTENANCE, AND RESURGENCE OF RESOURCE CONFLICTS

In the Niger Delta, there is a strong perception that Nigeria's political structure is tilted against the people of the region. As discussed in chapter 5, one of the dominant themes in this study concerns the perception that Nigeria's federalism operates contrary to the true spirit of a federation, and that the country's political structure is skewed against the oil-producing communities in the Niger Delta because these are minority groups. As perceived by the people of the Niger Delta, the country's political structure appears to favor the dominant ethnic groups. One argument says the federal government controls the natural resources and those who own the land from which the oil and gas are produced are, broadly speaking, excluded from the benefits. This, participants claim, is done through the enactment of decrees and constitutional adjustments by several military regimes that take away the ownership rights of the Niger Delta communities to oil and gas resources exploited in their territory. This is a huge conflict trigger and consistently arises in discussions, petitions, and writings. One participant proposes, as I discuss in chapter 5, that "political structure is acting as a conflict stimulus, resource conflict stimulus." It is appropriate at this juncture to recall the comments of participant Oloko510:

> Once the government discover oil and gas in your environment, on your land, you cease to be the owner of that land. That is deprivation of the highest order. And when they mine this oil and obtain all the moneys accruing to it, you are not considered as a stakeholder. And by the Nigerian constitution, government has the right to all the money that come from the mining of oil and gas and they reserve the decision as to where they should spend the money, what they should spend it on.[2]

Another participant, a community environmental campaigner, Golam250, previously cited in chapter 5, has a similar take:

> Military decrees like the petroleum act and the land use decree of 1978 were used by military governments in Nigeria to expropriate, to take away ownership from the rightful owners of the resources. And so, these are some of the constitutional or legal instruments through which ownership is denied our people. This practice is widespread in the oil industry where government official will remain in Abuja and give license to some persons to come to explore and exploit crude oil in the Niger Delta, without even the people that own the land being part of the agreement.[3]

Indeed, the salience of the argument requires a third perspective from a third participant, community activist, Lebon960:

> Among the community people, there is the ingrained sense of ownership, some inherent sense of ownership, a belief and conviction that the resources found in their land belong to them. And when the central government enacts a law that says the natural resources belong to the state that creates a crisis, tension within the community.[4]

The decision of the federal government to claim total ownership of crude oil is controversial and contentious and has been widely condemned as unfair and against natural justice by all sections of the people of the oil-producing Niger Delta. A former senator who represented Delta State during Nigeria's Second Republic (1979–1983), Senator930, expressed the following opinion:

> Just as the price of labor is wages, capital has interest, entrepreneurship is driven by profit while rent and royalties are rewards for land ownership. Rent is a return for the use of the original and indestructible properties of the soil. Whoever owns land expects some form of compensation from those hiring this very important factor of production. The clamor for resource control is a clamor for adequate compensation, a cry for the redistribution of the revenue allocation formula, and nothing more. The only thing the government should do is to impose tax to be used for the welfare of the community. (Dafinone, 2001, 30)

Another perspective regarding the assertion that political structure acts as a conflict stimulant is the allegation that the decision of the federal government to have exclusive control of natural resources only apply to oil and gas and not all other natural resources. In this vein, Senator930 argues that

> It is instructive to note that the exclusive federal jurisdiction over a natural resource applies only to oil and gas and not to cocoa, palm oil, hides and skin, bitumen, and marble. This is the core of the agitation of the people of the South-South Region (Niger Delta). (Dafinone, 2001, 31)

This government policy of declaring crude oil and gas as belonging to the government while other natural resources are not so designated is considered discriminatory against the Niger Delta people and is a constant source of conflict. In order to douse the tension between the government and the Niger Delta communities, a former vice-chancellor (the equivalent of president) of the University of Ibadan, the premier institution of higher learning in Nigeria, and a former senator representing Rivers West Constituency called for changes to the laws governing oil production to restore the rights of landowners and to end to pollution and lack of development. The vice-chancellor919 stated,

> It is imperative that the rights of ownership and control of resources be restored to the people of the area in which the resources are located. Then applicable taxes may be paid the government at the center. This is the only way through which the neglect of the Niger Delta would cease, and the agitations brought to an end. (Don-Pedro, 2001, 15)

Also, presenting a paper at a conference titled, *The Niger Delta: the Past, the Present and the Way Forward*, Senator929 suggested the repeal of laws governing the relationships between oil firms and the communities in which they carry out their operations, in favor of the communities in order to bring an end to environmental degradation and the near-total absence of basic amenities in most of the oil-bearing communities (Don-Pedro, 2001, 15).

There are five strands of thinking concerning how Niger Delta advocates view the country's political culture in causing and perpetuating conflicts. The most prevalent reason concerns the enactment of constitutional provisions that deny the people of the Niger Delta access, control, and management of the crude oil and gas resources exploited in their territory. To summarize this point, I paraphrase and rely on the work of Itse Sagay, a constitutional lawyer and a former Dean of the Faculty of Law, University of Benin, Delta State:

The following pieces of legislation enacted during the period 1969–1999 show how the minority peoples of the Niger Delta are deprived and marginalized of their petroleum resources:

Petroleum Decree 51 of 1969—Expropriated all petroleum resources from the oil-producing states and placed them under total federal government ownership.

- Off-shore Oil Revenue Decree (No. 9 of 1971)—All minerals in the continental shelves of coastal states were expropriated by the federal government. The decree repealed Section 140 (6) of the Constitution of the Federation which provides that the continental shelf of a state shall be deemed to be part of that state. Accordingly, (a) the ownership of and the title to the territorial waters and the continental shelf shall vest in the federal military government; and (b) all royalties, rents, and other revenues derived from or relating to the exploration, prospecting, or searching for or the winning of working petroleum (as defined in the Petroleum Decree, 1969) in the territorial waters and the continental shelf shall accrue to the federal military government.
- The Land Use Act, 1978—Transferred ownership of land from communities to the state governors, without compensation.
- Sections 40(3), 42(3) of the 1979, 1989, and 1999 Constitutions, respectively, restate the exclusive federal government ownership of the mineral resources of mineral-producing communities.
- Although the (i) Oil Pipeline Act 1965, (ii) the Petroleum Drilling and Production Decree 1969; and (iii) the Petroleum Decree of 1969 make provisions for compensation in cases of leakage, spillage, damage to surface rights or their mandatory acquisition thereof, in reality, these communities are left to bargain with the oil companies who exploit their weak economic

and legal positions to extort their consent to paltry compensation for lost land and natural resources.[5]

It must be noted that most of these legislations were enacted mostly by military regimes in the form of decrees and proclamations with little or no input from the communities or the local people. Prominent political figures have also made similar point although for differing reasons. Bisi Akande, a former interim National Chairman of the ruling APC and also a former governor of Osun State in a lecture "Devolution of Powers and National Restructuring" delivered at the APC-USA Second Annual Convention in Washington, D.C., in October 2018 blamed the military for Nigeria's lopsided political structure. Akande (2018) states,

> Successive military governments in the country between 1966 and 1999 were the architects of the current lopsided political structure in the country. The various military regimes created states and local governments solely for selfish reasons rather than through any scientific political reasoning. The military might have inequitably created more local governments per population per state in the North than in the South, thus giving the North an unfair advantage in revenue allocation from the national treasury. (Akande, 2018)

The second most prevalent line of reasoning concerns the formula for sharing federal revenue, particularly the weight of derivation. Advocates of the Niger Delta point to the sharing formula used in the 1960 and 1963 constitutions that allowed the regions to retain 50 percent of the revenue derived in that region. The formula was discarded when crude oil became the main revenue earner for the country. Both the 1960 and 1963 constitutions included the derivation principle in the formula for sharing revenue in Section 140 (1):

- Fifty percent proceeds of minerals, including mineral oil, be given to regions from which were extracted.
- Thirty percent went into the distributable pool (for all the regions including the producing region).
- Twenty percent for the federal government.
- Thirty percent of import duties went into the distributable pool.
- Import duty on petrol and diesel consigned to any region was refundable to that region. This also applied to excise duty on tobacco.

Given this formula, one can conclude that although the 1960 constitution did not provide for the ownership and control of mineral resources by the producing region or community, the entitlement of the producer region to 50 percent of the proceeds, and a share in another 30 percent with the federal government being entitled to only 20 percent was a true reflection of the derivative principle which is the economic indication of true federalism. Niger Delta youths complained that,

> The principle of derivation in revenue allocation has been consciously and systematically obliterated by successive regimes of the Nigerian State. We note the drastic reduction of derivation principle from 100 percent (1953), 50 percent (1960), 45 percent (1970), 20 percent (1975), 2 percent (1982), 1.5 percent (1984), and 3 percent (1992). (Don-Pedro, 2001, 20)

I must quickly add here that the derivation principle was raised to 13 percent in 2000 due to agitations from the Niger Delta and it has remained at 13 percent ever since.

The third strand of thought is the argument that political power holders have enacted discriminatory laws and policies to deprive the minority people of the Niger Delta of the resources produced in their environment. Thus, it is argued that by declaring crude oil and gas as belonging to the government while other mineral resources are not so designated, government shows bias and blatant discrimination against the Niger Delta people and is a constant source of conflict.

The fourth strand of thought entails the argument that creation of states and local governments whittles down the powers of states as compares to the regions. The federal government continues to acquire more powers and financial strength. Whereas during the period Nigeria was divided into regions, each region had its own constitution, in addition to the national constitution, a coat of arms, and motto, had its own semi-independent mission in the United Kingdom, and controlled 50 percent of the income derived from its territory, those constitutional powers were eliminated with the petroleum decree of 1969.

The fifth strand of thought argues that there is no avenue for the people of the Niger Delta, being minorities and lacking political clout, to undo the decrees and military legislations. The people feel powerless. In the current democratic dispensation, passing a bill or overturning unpopular legislation, for example, creating new states or local government requires two-thirds majority support from the existing states, a requirement that is considered a real tall order.

The foregoing aligns with the literature as Alao (2007) observes,

> For the people of the Niger Delta, the treatment from successive federal governments ties in with the aforementioned theme of politics of revenue allocation in the country. This is viewed as being grossly unfair since they produce the main commodity responsible for the majority of the country's external earnings. A

> look at the history of derivation and revenue allocation show the diminishing returns to the oil-producing regions. . . . This pattern instills in the people of Nigeria's oil-producing regions the impression of unfair treatment. The reward being sought from the struggle is an increase in the derivation allocated to them. (p. 174)

I have shown in this section that through a combination enactment of military decrees, constitutional provisions, policy adjustments, revenue sharing formulas, and government practices, Nigeria's political structure is perceived as unfair, discriminatory, and tilted against the interests of the Niger Delta people. Specifically, the transfer of ownership of the natural resources, crude oil, and gas from the communities to the federal government triggers discontent, bitterness, and anger in the Niger Delta. These feelings and grievances contribute to the sustenance and resurgence of conflicts in the Niger Delta.

THE WAYS MOBILIZATION METHODS OF CONFLICT ACTORS AFFECT THE RELATIONSHIP BETWEEN TRANSNATIONAL OIL CORPORATIONS AND OIL-PRODUCING COMMUNITIES

Oil-producing companies have had frosty relationships with host communities. The perception of oil-producing communities is that adopting peaceful means of mobilization does not appear to have beneficial returns in the short term. As indicated in chapter 5 and earlier in this chapter, oil prospecting started during the colonial era during which period oil-producing and host communities had little understanding and knowledge about crude oil production. The colonial authorities and the succeeding post-independence administrations made the communities sign off their rights and privileges during unfair and lopsided negotiations, which left the communities holding the short end of the stick. Saro-Wiwa (1992) commented about this before he launched the peaceful mobilization of Ogoni people against oil companies operating in the area in 1990:

> It has to be said that at that time, the Nigerian government knew pretty little of the oil industry. There were not enough trained men in the relevant supervising ministries of the government to draft the laws and regulations which would bind Shell-BP to minimum standards of civilized behavior. Shell-BP consequently seized upon this fact and displayed the ugliest possible face of international capitalism. Operating among a peasant population which, as this study has shown, knew little of the ways of the modern world, Shell-BP has behaved cruelly, stupidly, and in a racist manner. (p. 44)

One of the themes that emerged from the participant interviews relative to the issue of mobilization of conflict actors and response of IOCs is the universal assertion that the government and the IOCs tend to resort to the use of heavy violence against community protests and agitations even when these agitations are peaceful and nonviolent. Participants frequently cited the violent put down of the peaceful protest of the people of Etche in Rivers by Shell Oil that occurred in 1990, an incident that I have previously studied. They also recall the pacification of the Ogoni struggle and eventual hanging of Saro-Wiwa and eight other Ogoni activists in November 1990 as examples of violent state responses to legitimate demands of the people of the Niger Delta for justice.

Participants argue that the nature of the Nigerian state is a very patently violent state and its response to most of these issues have been quite violent. And that even if groups organize themselves nonviolently, the response has been the frequent resort to violence on the part of the government and on the part of the oil companies. It is pertinent to add here that in the Umuechem incident referenced above, 80 people and 495 houses were allegedly burned and seriously damaged. Those allegedly killed by the police included Pastor Sunday Ukonu of the Apostolic Church, Umuechem, and the Chief A. A. Ordu, the traditional ruler of the community and his two sons, as well as eight other villagers who sought refuge in the chief's compound.[6]

A significant theme from my finding is that the contentious relationship between the oil-producing communities and the IOCs reflect the history, years of interaction, and their shared experiences. Distrust set in due to the way members of the local communities are perceived and allegedly treated with disdain by the IOCs and the government. Several participants alluded to this point. Participant Alale310 recalls,

> Over the years the community people have many times been shortchanged by the government and oil companies. When anyone comes around to do anything, even with good intention, they see you as part of the oppressors that have come to shortchange them too.[7]

Mobilization in the Niger Delta could be seen in three phases.

- During the first phase, peaceful means—petitions, vigils, arbitrations, filing lawsuits, rallies, and peaceful protests were utilized to highlight the grievances of individual and isolated villages and communities. These were isolated cases of villages that host oil companies attempting to channel their grievances in the ways they knew how. In the case of the Ogoni people, Saro-Wiwa recall that petitions and peaceful demonstrations were carried out by students, citizens, and chiefs of Kegbara Dere, Bomu, and

Ebubu and against Shell Oil shortly after the Nigerian civil war (Saro-Wiwa, 1992).

- Community organizing—MOSOP and other community groups during the period 1990–1993 engaged in coordinated and organized campaigns utilizing nonviolent methods as outlined above to mobilize their people against perceived injustices including environmental pollution (Omotola, 2009; Osaghae, 2008). This is the second phase. Saro-Wiwa used prayer, vigils, one Naira fund, church services, peaceful rallies and demonstrations, a proliferation of community organizations that hold regular meetings, issue of an ultimatum (demand notice), press briefings, interviews, a boycott of the presidential election on June 12, 1993, networking with NGOs and international organizations (Greenpeace, Human Rights Watch, Amnesty International, Pen International), and using international instruments at the United Nations including UN Working Group on Indigenous peoples, UN Committee on the Eradication of Racial Discrimination, and annual meetings of the United Nations Human Rights Commission, Geneva, to mobilize the Ogoni and call the attention of the international community to the plight of his people. Mobilization exposed the ills and the shortcomings of the IOCS especially when their practices or *modus operandi* in the Niger Delta are compared with those obtainable in the industrialized, western countries. Mobilization sort of opens the eyes of the people of the Niger Delta to their rights, responsibilities, and possibilities.
- The third phase of mobilization entails an analysis of the responses of the Nigerian state and IOCs. As indicated in the introductory chapter and throughout this study, it has been established through research that the Nigerian government and the IOCs have the habit of using overwhelming force and brutality to crush community agitations even when they are done peacefully. A number of studies have highlighted some of the responses of the Nigerian state and the oil companies to the agitations and protests of the Niger Delta communities all of which involved the use of heavy violence (Frynas, 2001; Ibeanu, 2000; Manby, 1999; Okonta & Douglas, 2001; Osaghae, 2008; Pegg, 1999; Ukiwo, 2007). Prominent among these cases are those of Umuechem (1990), Ogoni (1993–1995) in Rivers State, and Odi (2001) in Bayelsa State. Ibeanu, (2000), Omotola (2009), and Osaghae (2008) did extensive studies on mobilization of community agitators and the specific responses of the state and the oil companies, pointing out the central role of the IOCs in the power equation.

Ibeanu's (2000) perspective is appropriate here:

> Shell remains the largest producer in Nigeria . . . inevitably, this position has brought Shell very close to the ruling governments in Nigeria. In fact, for many

> communities in the Niger Delta, there is little difference between the oil companies, especially Shell, and the Nigerian state. This assumption is not entirely without justification. For instance, on countless occasions, oil companies have called out directly the police, the army, and the navy to quell disturbances on their installations, without applying to the government for help. (pp. 21–22)

Political leaders in the Niger Delta also took advantage of the struggle to demand more revenue, appointments, access, and relevance. The governors of six minority oil-producing states in the Niger Delta, for example, (Akwa Ibom, Bayelsa, Cross River, Delta, Edo, and Rivers) had a meeting in Benin City, Delta State, in 2000 and added their voice to the demand for resource control by their citizens (Isumonah, 2015). One of the governors stated that "they joined the demand for resource control train when their demand for the implementation of the minimum 13 percent derivation principle provided for and enshrined in Section 162 (2) of the constitution of the Federal Republic of Nigeria 1999, was ignored by the federal government" (Isumonah, 2015, 649).

Insurgency

The fourth phase refers to the era of insurgency. While some commentaries have suggested that the turn to militancy and insurgency in the Niger Delta was due to greed or the desire for personal enrichment on the part of militants, Demirel-Pegg and Pegg (2015) argue that a more compelling explanation is the perceived failure of nonviolent methods and collective action. In a study of the rise of militancy among the Ijaw in and around Warri in Delta, Ukiwo (2007) also argues that communities turned to violence only after repeated failure of oil companies to respond to petitions and other peaceful means of demand. Thus, Ijaw communities learned that the same oil companies that brazenly ignored peaceful protests, "responded speedily, under threat of violence and 'direct action,' to community demands" (Ukiwo, 2007, 609).

The implication of this policy choice is that "Ijaw youths have come to realize that the only language government and oil companies understand is violence" (Ukiwo, 2007, 609). In a similar report, the International Crisis Group (2006) observes that militants have "learned the unfortunate lesson that violence, extortion and kidnaping are a way—sometimes the only way—to be taken seriously" (p. 1).

Critical to understanding the scope, depth, and ramifications of the demands of the oil-producing communities in the Niger Delta is the fact that they all dovetail from the original arguments advanced by Saro-Wiwa in 1990. The mobilization techniques of the MOSOP changed the perception of the oil-bearing communities toward the government and the IOCs by articulating the possible ways their grievances would be addressed (Isumonah, 2015; Omotola, 2009; Osaghae, 2008).

To improve the relationship between oil-producing communities, a former senator who represented Rivers State, Senator929 previously cited above, has suggested the repeal of laws governing the relationships between oil firms and the communities in which they carry out their operations, in favor of the communities in order to bring an end to environmental degradation and the near-total absence of basic amenities in most of the oil-bearing communities.

Before I conclude this section, I must add at this juncture that some of the IOCs have reported that they have increased the funds allocated to community development assistance in response to community agitations. And that they began new initiatives to improve relations with host communities by signing MOUs with them and also by working through CSOs, CBOs, and peace advocates, and also through increases in the use of corporate responsibility programs. Some communities and CBOs, however, dispute some of the claims of development assistance by the IOCs (Demirel-Pegg & Pegg, 2015).

In summary, there is enduring distrust and suspicion between oil-producing communities and the oil companies that conduct oil exploration activities in their territories. Methods of mobilization, which entail peaceful, violent, and a mixture of both methods, have led to further escalation of distrust, disaffection, and conflict in most instances. Given the contribution of oil revenue to the federal government treasury, the oil companies retain significant influence such that they frequently resort to engaging the security services to crackdown on community agitations rather than negotiate with the local people to resolve differences.

A significant implication or fallout of the mobilization of Saro-Wiwa and MOSOP is that the people of the Niger Delta now use the grievances, the arguments advanced by Saro-Wiwa and his followers as benchmarks against which they could measure if the government and the IOCs have addressed or made any progress toward addressing their complaints.

RESOURCE GOVERNANCE AND ITS IMPACT ON PROTRACTED CONFLICTS IN NIGERIA'S NIGER DELTA

In the following paragraphs, I provide answers to my main research question by discussing the findings and themes that emerged from the data as demonstrated during the review of the subsidiary questions. How does resource governance impact protracted social conflicts in Nigeria's Niger Delta? Resource governance has the most significant impact on the protracted social conflicts in the Niger Delta. This can be examined or discussed in several ways.

First, let us review the dominant themes as discussed both in chapter 5 and in this chapter. The dominant theme that emerged from the data presentation is the perception that resource governance has the most significant impact on the continuity, elongation, and sporadic outburst of conflict in Nigeria's Niger Delta. Most of the participants, twenty-nine out of thirty or 96.67 percent suggest that resource government accounts for the persistence of resource conflicts in the Niger Delta. One participant, Prof. Olule840, reflects:

> Resource governance is at the center of the entire Niger Delta conflicts. Governance is at the fulcrum, is at the center; it is at the middle of the entire conflicts in the Niger Delta regarding oil exploration. And the question might be, how? Think of governance in terms of, we have natural resources, crude oil, and gas here in this region. Now, who are those who control and administer these resources? Do the Niger Delta people control and administer these resources? No, they do not! That is the anger of the people.[8]

Also expressing similar sentiments, a female participant, one of six female respondents, participant PeaceLady950, proposes that

> The major cause of conflicts in the Niger Delta has been centered on resource ownership, management, and extraction issues around them. We have had situations where communities that are relatively peaceful but once crude oil is found, and extraction activities begin we found out that the reverse is now the case.[9]

Second, the NIIA research collection on the Niger Delta conflicts, which I discussed in detail in chapter 5, identifies six aspects of resource governance frequently discussed in the media as having the most impact on the triggering and continuation of conflicts in the region. These include resource control (9.16 percent), Ogoni crisis (8.54 percent), resource ownership/land rights (7.91 percent), revenue allocation/revenue allocation formula (7.70 percent), derivation principle (7.30 percent), and environmental pollution (7.08 percent). The six perspectives of resource governance constitute some 47.69 percent of the discussions out of a total of twenty categories compiled by the NIIA.

Third, Nigeria's current vice president recently joined the debate on resource governance in a town hall meeting in Minnesota during a visit to the United States, VP910, and recalls,

> I served as Attorney General in Lagos State and one of the chief issues that we fought in Lagos state was what you call fiscal federalism. We felt that there was a need for the states to be stronger, for states to, more or less, determine their fortunes. So, for example, we went to court to contest the idea that every state

> should control, to a certain extent, its own resources (the so-called resource control debate). We were in court at that time up to the Supreme Court and the court ruled that oil-producing states should continue to get 13% derivation. While we were at the Supreme Court only the oil-producing states and Lagos were interested in resource control, everybody else was not interested in resource control for obvious reasons. (Agbakwuru, 2018, 1)

Fourth, the literature on the Niger Delta identifies politics and dominant systems of governance as core ingredients of conflict in the region (Williams, 2011). Here are the relevant thoughts of Williams (2011):

> The crucial underlying factor was the corrupt political relationships which made up what Watts called Nigeria's "oil complex"—the murky alliances between local political, military and business elites, transnational firms that represent the global oil industry, and a variety of foreign governments which turned a blind eye to the whole sordid process. (p. 87)

My findings identify three major critical layers of actors and their attendant agendas and networks in the Niger Delta conflict. These are the government, the IOCs, and the oil-producing communities. The presence of IOCs, their employees, and facilities have significant negative impacts on the livelihood and way of life of the local population. The most significant changes among the conflict actors are seen in the protagonists and advocates of reforms in the Niger Delta—most of the activists are youthful elements, including women, who now bear arms and adopt a violent approach. The youthful actors are much more aggressive and apparently elect to use violent means in the struggle as opposed to the early days of mature activists who preferred the peaceful and nonviolent approach. The dissatisfaction with the current governance mechanism or the absence of acceptable governance mechanism has invariably birthed the resort to violence by Niger Delta youth. The Nigeria Minister of State for Petroleum Resources announced in February 2017 that the country lost $100 billion in oil revenue in 2016 due to attacks by militants in the Niger Delta and that oil production fell by as much as one million barrels a day in the same year.

In addition, the majority of participants in a Gallup poll, the data from Nigeria Watch, and NIIA media research on the Niger Delta, earlier discussed in this chapter, all point to the conclusion that perception of deprivation and marginalization fuel conflict. All this help to provide answers to my central research question, how does resource governance impact protracted resource conflicts in Nigeria's Niger Delta? Current governance mechanisms negatively impact protracted resource conflicts in the Niger Delta as they invite so much criticism, disapproval, condemnation, and protests from the Niger

Delta so much so that there are frequent calls from all sections of the Niger Delta for reforms and mitigation. Resource governance or the failure of it as it connects to feeling of neglect, deprivation, and marginalization is a conflict trigger in the Niger Delta.

Regarding political structure, Niger Delta communities perceive Nigeria's political system as being unfair, discriminatory, and tilted against their interests. There is widespread perception that the federal government controls the natural resources and that those whose land produce crude oil and gas are excluded from the benefits. Government action is perceived to be exercised through the enactment of decrees and constitutional adjustment by several military regimes that take away the ownership rights of the Niger Delta communities to oil and gas resources exploited in their territory. This is perceived as a conflict propeller and consistently arises in discussions, petitions, and writings.

The decision of the central government to claim ownership of crude oil is controversial and contentious and has been widely condemned as unfair and against natural justice by all sections of the Niger Delta. This decision is seen as a conflict stimulant as it is alleged that the exclusive control of natural resources by the federal government only applies to oil and gas and not to all other natural resources like cocoa, palm oil, hides and skin, bitumen, and marble. These perceptions help me to answer my main research question, how does resource governance impact protracted resource conflicts in Nigeria's Niger Delta? Nigeria's distorted political structure fuels or heightens resource conflicts in the Niger Delta. Conversely, if reforms are initiated that are perceived to address these negative perceptions, they would help ease tension and deescalate conflicts.

Regarding mobilization and relationship between oil-producing communities and oil companies, my findings helped me to answer my main research, how does resource governance impact protracted resource conflicts in Nigeria's Niger Delta? First, the relationship between oil-producing communities and the IOCs fall within governance issues related to ownership, extraction, management, and sharing of natural resources in Nigeria. Other matters that fall within the scope of resource governance include environment pollution, gas flaring, and oil spills. Second, the incessant and persistent friction between oil-producing companies and IOCs exemplify how resource governance negatively impacts the peace of the Niger Delta. What is needed to improve community-IOC relationship is clear policy initiative that spells out in clear terms the relationship between oil-producing communities and IOCs such that the interests of the Niger Delta people are taken into consideration and protected.

I have shown in the foregoing sections that resource governance constitutes the most significant impact on the manifestation of resource conflicts in Nigeria's Niger Delta and that mitigation efforts must focus on addressing the grievances and perceptions of the people. Most of the issues and topics analyzed as impacting conflicts in the Niger Delta emanate from and revolve around resource governance. In the next chapter I turn to discuss the lessons and takeaways of this study.

NOTES

1. Personal interview, Port Harcourt, Rivers State, November 2017.
2. Personal interview, Bodo, Rivers State, Nigeria, November 2017.
3. Personal interview, Yenegoa, Bayelsa State, Nigeria, December 2017.
4. Personal interview, Bodo, Rivers State, Nigeria, November 2017.
5. Itse Sagay, Nigeria, Federalism, the Constitution, and Resource Control, *The Guardian Newspaper*, May 21, 2001, 30–31.
6. Additional details available in the final published report of the Commission of Inquiry into the Umuechem Massacre instituted by Col. Godwin Osagie Abbe, the Military Governor of Rivers State in 1991.
7. Personal Interview, Port Harcourt, Nigeria, November 2017.
8. Personal interview, Port Harcourt, Rivers State, Nigeria, December 2017.
9. Personal interview, Yenegoa, Bayelsa, State, Nigeria, November 2017.

Chapter 7

Lessons and Takeaways for Leaders and the Rest of Us

DE-ESCALATION

Reforms targeted at current governance mechanisms will aid in resolving the Niger Delta conflicts. If there is political will and genuine intent among the political leaders in Nigeria to systematically and strategically seek and proffer solutions and remedies to the grievances and complaints by the Niger Delta communities, with input from a wide range of conflict actors and stakeholders, the protracted resource conflicts in the region could be transformed. My study participants point to the demonstrated action of President Yar'Adua who introduced the amnesty program in 2009. The program was initially hugely controversial and unpopular especially among political leaders in northern Nigeria. It was perceived as rewarding criminality and subversion. But as the amnesty program gradually led to the reduction of violence against oil companies and the restoration of full-scale oil production, opposition to it began to wane.

LOOKING AHEAD

Given that my research questions emerged from robust literature review, and the resource governance and Azar's theoretical framework, and based on my findings, I make the following suggestions to the following audiences connected to my theory—community, lack of development/relative deprivation, state/political structure, and international linkages/oil companies/environment.

COMMUNITY

The oil-producing communities in the Niger Delta should recognize that while the dominant influence and the identities of the traditional actors and stakeholders such as the government, oil companies like Shell Oil, ExxonMobil, and Chevron continue, youthful actors in the communities who now bear arms and operate underground have altered the dynamic of struggle. This recommendation resonates with the literature and the theoretical framework of this study. Williams (2011) states that resources did not extract themselves and sell themselves, it is done by actors.

LACK OF DEVELOPMENT/RELATIVE DEPRIVATION

The absence of basic social amenities in the Niger Delta, especially in the oil-producing villages and those who host oil infrastructure and facilities, continues to baffle and intrigue the local indigenes, and first-time visitors to the Niger Delta. As indicated in chapter 6, this backwardness of the oil-producing communities contrasts with the oil camps just a few miles away that boast of the modern amenities of life. Government, transnational oil companies, international agencies, and philanthropic organizations should, as a matter of priority, pool resources together to provide social amenities to the local people. Community agitations should also target the state and local governments to devote financial resources to local development.

STATE/POLITICAL STRUCTURES

Government should look into the complaints from the Niger Delta communities, specifically the legislation that takes away ownership to a piece of land from a farmer or landowner immediately crude oil is discovered on the land. Reforms and measures that seek to address land rights, resource control, and community participation should be discussed and implemented. Similarly, any decree or legislation that usurp the rights of the local people or exclude oil-producing from the benefits of crude oil resources should be researched and reviewed by government with the intention to introduce reforms. Here I reproduce an expert opinion again. Participant Zima450 suggests:

> Government need to put up a new framework to include all actors and stakeholders to brainstorm in a conducive environment on the conflicts. The process and the discussion should not be skewed to the advantage of any particular actors or stakeholders. This proposed framework must be all-encompassing, inclusive,

participatory, just, and sustainable. The framework should be designed around the actors and the multifaceted dimensions of resource conflicts in the Niger Delta. It is only when all actors and stakeholders bring their issues and interests to the table, to consider their merits, could a formidable framework be negotiated.[1]

INTERNATIONAL OIL COMPANIES/ CLIMATE CHANGE LINKAGES/ TRANSNATIONAL /INDIGENOUS RIGHTS

The dominant role and influence of transnational oil companies in Nigeria's economy, the impact of their activities on the livelihood and traditional occupations of the local people, and the distortions that the oil industry has caused require immediate mitigation. Oil spills, gas flaring, and oil exploration dislocations have caused greenhouse effects, acid rain, and environment damage as documented by the 2011 UNEP on Ogoniland. Climate change is real in the Niger Delta, the region is reporting hotter temperature and unprecedented flooding during the last two years.

MOSOP and the Environmental Rights Action, a local Nigerian environmental advocacy group affiliated with Friends of the Earth, have for several years appeared before the United Nations Working Group on Indigenous Peoples and other international forums to call attention to the threats posed by oil production to the livelihood of the Ogoni and other indigenous groups in the Niger Delta. Indeed, the Ogoni chose to use "survival" in the name of their advocacy group due to the concern that oil production could destroy them from the face of the earth. In summary, the UNEP report should be implemented without delay.

The challenge with the above recommendations is that they are still dependent on the government or government agencies doing the right thing. Finally, the recommendations speak to Azar's theoretical position that identifies "governance and the state role" as the critical factor in the satisfaction or frustration of individual and identity group needs as well as the centrality of conflict actors and stakeholders.

POLICY IMPLICATIONS

My findings and recommendations have transformational implications for policymakers, government officials, executives of transnational oil companies, traditional rulers, and opinion leaders in the oil-bearing communities. Broadly speaking, the findings could facilitate and assist decision-makers and government to focus and channel their resources toward the specific issues and grievances that attracted the most complaints from the conflict actors and participants.

The issue of conflict of interest regarding the role of the Nigerian government is a significant contribution to literature from this study. The government is a joint partner with the IOCs owning 55–60 percent equity of the oil majors codified by a JV agreement. It is important to recall the assertion of participant Zima450 who says,

> Unfortunately, the Nigerian government is both an investor and a protector, which is a conflict of interest. You cannot be an investor in the business of oil production and at the same time you are saddled with the responsibility of ensuring that the entire value chain of oil and gas production in the country is done in a credible and transparent manner. No, it will not work.[2]

This participant's concern is at the core of the conflict in the Niger Delta as the reference is to the business relationship the Nigerian government has with the IOCs operating in the region. A third party or group of third-party negotiators seen as neutral and fair-minded and with a track record of integrity will go a lot to build trust and facilitate negotiations.

Crucially significant and helpful to the key actors, especially the government, the IOCs, and the oil-bearing communities, are findings related to the changes that have taken place in the identities, influence, and operations of informal groups and youth networks in the Niger Delta during the two decades of conflict. These changes and the reasons given are critical to any proposed reforms that the government and the IOCs would be willing to consider in transforming the conflict.

Equally important and useful are the findings and recommendations pertaining to the desire of the oil-bearing communities to participate, to feel that they are giving opportunities to participate in the oil industry, to feel a sense of belonging, to have some access to the crude oil resources in land.

One example of positive impact identified by participants is the increase of derivation principle in the revenue sharing formula from 1.5 percent to 13 percent in 1999. Five participants, or 16.66 percent of respondents, point out that this was due to pressure and the agitation of the oil-producing communities and only came after the oil-producing states and Lagos took the federal government to the Supreme Court. The highest court of the land ruled in favor of the plaintiffs. The court decision resulted in the oil-producing states receiving additional 117.9 million Naira in derivation funds out of the total crude oil earnings of 7.815 billion Naira in fiscal year 1982 (Ndujihe, 2016).

All this demonstrates that, on the ground, a potential exists that a comprehensive peace strategy could emerge in the future, especially when none of the key actors has discountenanced the option for dialogue even though they might pay lip service to the peace process. This assertion does not in any way ignore the simmering discontent, deep-seated frustration, and palpable anger that are on full display among the ordinary citizens of the Niger Delta.

LIMITATIONS OF THE STUDY

This work does not study all the aspects of the Niger Delta crisis. My research does not assess the effectiveness of specific governance initiatives that the Nigerian government might have introduced in response to the decades of conflicts in the Niger Delta. My focus is limited to analyzing the Niger Delta conflicts from the perspectives that emerged in the literature about resource governance as well as the theoretical propositions on protracted social conflicts.

Inquiry measured perceptions and has a limited pool of interviewees. Fieldwork interviews were conducted in Port Harcourt in Rivers State and Yenegoa in Bayelsa State and data collections took place in Lagos and Abuja. Opportunities for additional interviews in Delta State arose in the field but the prospect for an elevated security threat level against the researcher was too high and I made the decision to not conduct interviews in that section of the Niger Delta. Due to financial constraints, fieldwork was done in three months.

Areas for Future Research

Based on the findings presented in this study, I hereby in this section discuss and summarize areas of further research. The proposed issues for study could possibly unearth and yield useful and important perspectives regarding resource governance, protracted social conflict, and the resolution of the Niger Delta conflicts.

First, it should be revealing to investigate how the Nigerian government and the transnational oil companies have attempted to build a relationship with the many Niger Delta communities in which they operate. Such an inquiry would focus on trust-related issues between the key actors and stakeholders. This is necessary as trust-related comments arose several times among the participants and in the data during my field research in Bayelsa and Rivers states. Trust-related issues were not the focus on my study, although I made references to it.

Second, one related line of inquiry would be to compare resource governance mechanisms in Nigeria with another possible African or developing oil-producing nation to see how they fare, and to study their similarities and differences.

Third, it would be interesting to find out the level of success achieved by some of the recent policy rolled out by the government in response to pressures and protests by activists in the Niger Delta and their sympathizers. Nigeria's current Minister of State for Petroleum Resources, the government department responsible for the oil industry, in February 2017 released a twenty-point agenda, titled "Oil Sector Militancy Challenges: Roadmap to Closure," designed to end militancy and stop the loss of oil revenue and the decline in oil production figures. Some of the measures the minister outlined include "engagement town hall meetings, inter-agency collaboration, ring-fenced state approach, security hold hands, peace and investment on state basis, focused investments in gas-to-power, incentive for peace scheme, massive civil infrastructure revamp, and Niger Delta Development Fund."[3] How effective has the government been in implementing these far-reaching proposals would be interesting to investigate.

Finally, a key issue of study would be a focus on how the absence of environmental protection mechanisms, or the failure to enforce them, affects the livelihood of the people in the host communities in relation to changes in climate and weather conditions over the years. In view of international focus on climate change, especially given that research has shown that oil production in Nigeria has contributed to greenhouse effects, such investigation is long overdue. In the last chapter, I make my conclusive remarks.

NOTES

1. Personal interview, Port Harcourt, Rivers State, Nigeria, November 2017.
2. Personal interview, Port Harcourt, Rivers State, Nigeria, November 2017.
3. See additional details in *Economic Confidential*, February 2018 issue.

Conclusion

The natural resource conflict in the Niger Delta is complex, and multifaceted. The conflict emerged in the early 1990s and has since escalated and become intractable. It attracted international attention in 1995, when Ken Saro-Wiwa, who led the Ogoni people to peacefully protest what they called environmental degradation by Shell, political marginalization, and economic strangulation by the government, was hanged with eight other Ogoni activists.

Understanding the protracted conflicts associated with the production of crude oil in Nigeria's Niger Delta region requires a deep appreciation for and understanding of the history, the culture, the environment, the struggles, the perceptions, and the grievances of the Niger Delta people in relation to the larger politics of the Nigerian federation.

Understanding, addressing, and resolving these conflicts would fundamentally require regular and consistent review, iteration, and targeted measures to meet the demands of the Niger Delta communities, and fulfill Nigeria's national and international obligations. Given the size and population of Nigeria and the significant contribution of the oil and gas sector to federal government revenue, agitations for resource control or greater access to the oil revenue in the Niger Delta is seen, in some quarters, as a security threat or threat to the well-being and stability of the country and have been met with high-scale crackdown by the federal authorities.

In this study, natural resources in the broadest sense is referencing crude oil and gas resources exploited and produced in Nigeria's Niger Delta, the mainstay of the Nigerian economy. This study has been divided into seven chapters. In chapter 1, I introduced and provided a general overview of the study. In this chapter, I discussed the rationale for the study and the research questions. Focusing on conflicts associated with oil production and the distribution of proceeds from petroleum rents, royalties, and taxes among the constituents' units in the Nigerian federation, I inquired why the conflicts have persisted. Admitting that many studies have been done on the Niger Delta, I established that those studies did not address the protracted character of the conflicts between the local communities, transnational oil corporations, and the federal government, especially the resurgence of conflicts and the emergence of new actors, particularly youthful militant actors, such as the NDA in 2016. Hence, a compelling need to examine the severity, intensity, and longevity of the conflicts.

In chapter 2, I discussed the background and historical context of the study, providing in-depth political and economic background on Nigeria, the Niger Delta, and its people. I believe that it was necessary to not only understand the events, developments, and personalities that have shaped the history of this region, but it was also important to highlight their contexts. Thus, I discussed the precolonial societies, the slave trade, the palm oil trade or "legitimate trade," colonial Nigeria, the agitations for creation of states by the people of this region before independence, the uprising of Isaac Boro, Ken Saro-Wiwa's nonviolent mobilization of the Ogoni people against the oil companies and the government through the instrument of MOSOP, and the Kaiama declaration of Ijaw youths. The agitations of the Niger Delta turned violent after the execution of Saro-Wiwa in 1995. The Avengers, who claimed that they were "young, educated and well-traveled," became highly active in late 2016 and 2017 and criticized the older militant groups for kidnapping people, killing soldiers, and enriching themselves. Promising to only attack oil infrastructure, they claimed to be better armed than the older groups of militants and have members from different ethnic groups and regions. The NDA also invoked the plight of the Ogoni and demanded greater ownership of oil resources for the people who live in crude-producing areas, environmental mitigation, compensation for damages inflicted by oil producers, and continued funding for the amnesty program.

In chapter 3, "Understanding the Nexus between Resource Governance, the State, and Protracted Conflict," I discuss the content of resource governance as an analytical tool, which, I argue, presents the most convincing propositions that capture the key elements that are critical to managing resource conflicts—the political systems, social relations, stakeholders and actors, elite networks, institutions, and regulations governing them.

In chapter 4, "Six Cardinal Pillars of Resource Governance," my study isolates what I would like to call *six cardinal pillars of resource governance*, namely, land rights, (resource control), revenue sharing, Nigeria's political structure, oil companies versus oil-producing communities relations, provision of basic amenities, and environmental pollution and mitigation. Any policy measures proposed to address the grievances of the Niger Delta should be targeted at these six pillars.

In chapter 5, "In the Eyes of the People," I discussed the perceptions and grievances of the people of the Niger Delta, exploring deep-seated, heartfelt perspectives and burdens of the people including their experiences of the communities in interaction with IOCs and the government.

In chapter 6, "The Heart of the Matter: The Ideal Place to Seek Solutions," I discuss and provide answers to inquiries about why the conflicts continue to linger after two decades. Policy makers and researchers interested in understanding and proffering solutions to the Niger Delta conflicts would need to pay attention to the complex nature of resource governance and its impact on conflict in the region. Key finding, as stated earlier, is that resource governance is at both the heart of conflict and the ideal place to find solutions. These conclusions resonate with literature and my theoretical framework. As Alao (2007, 35) states, "it is the failure of the states to effectively integrate all the contents of resource governance that is at the root of conflicts."

Finally, as discussed in chapter 7, "Lessons and Takeaways for Leaders and the Rest of Us," there has to be a genuine commitment and demonstration of intent to work toward resolution of the Niger Delta conflict by all the stakeholders—the government, the IOCs, and the oil-producing communities. The perceptions and grievances of the oil-producing communities as documented in this work need to be addressed with appropriate policy mechanisms to deescalate and mitigate the crises in the region.

Bibliography

Adamolekun, L. (2005). The Nigerian federation at the crossroads: the way forward. *Publius: The Journal of Federalism*, *35*(3), 383–405.

Adebayo, A. G. (19 93). *Embattled Federalism History of Revenue Allocation in Nigeria, 1946–1990*. New York, NY: Peter Lang Publishing, Inc.

Adegbami, A. (2013). Resource control and revenue allocation problems in Nigeria: implication for national peace. *American International Journal of Research in Humanities, Arts and Social Sciences*, *3*(1), 141–148.

Afeno, S. O. (2014). Killings by the security forces in Nigeria: mapping and trend analysis (2006–2014). *Nigeria Watch Project*. IFRA-Nigeria, Working Paper Series, 37, 1–45.

Agbakwuru, J. (2018, August 27). Nigeria's problem not restructuring – Osinbajo, *Vanguard Newspaper*. Retrieved from https://www.vanguardngr.com/

Akande, B. (2018, October 21). Blame Military for Lopsided Political Structure, *The Nation Newspape*r, Nigeria. Retrieved from https://thenationonlineng.net/?s=blame+military+for+lopsided+political+structure+-+Akande

Ako, R. T., & Okonmah, P. (2009). Minority rights issues in Nigeria: A theoretical analysis of historical and contemporary conflicts in the oil-rich Niger delta region. *International Journal on Minority and Group Rights*, *16*(1), 53–65.

Akpan, N. U. (1971). *The Struggle for Secession*. London, UK: Frank Cass.

Alao, A. (2007). *Natural resources and conflict in Africa: The tragedy of endowment*. Rochester, NY: University of Rochester Press.

Azar, E. (1990). *The management of Protracted Social Conflict: Theory and cases*. Hampshire, CT: Dartmouth.

Babalola, D. (2015). The efficacy of federalism in a multi-ethnic: Nigerian experience. *The Journal of Pan African Studies*, *8*(2), 74–91.

Birnbaum, M. (1995). *A Travesty of Law and Justice: An Analysis of the Judgement in the Case of Ken Saro-Wiwa and Others*. London, UK: Article 19 International Center Against Censorship.

Boro, I. A. (1982). *The Twelve-Day Revolution*. Benin, Nigeria: Iddo Umeh Publishers.

Burton, J. (1987). *Resolving Deep-Rooting Conflict: A handbook*. Lanham, MD: University Press of America.

Burton, J. (1990). *Conflict: Resolution and prevention*. New York, NY: St. Martins.

CIA Factbook. (2019). Country facts and figures. Colombia and Venezuela. United States Central Intelligence Agency. Retrieved from https://www.cia.gov/library/publications/the-world-factbook/geos/ve.html

Coleman, P. T. (2006). Intractable conflict. In M. Deutsch, P. T. Coleman, & E. C. Marcus (eds.), *The handbook of Conflict Resolution: theory and practice* (pp. 533–559). San Francisco, CA: John Wiley & Sons Inc.

Dafinone, D. (2001, April 8). Resource control: The economic and political dimensions. *The Guardian on Sunday*, pp. 30–31.

Demirel-Pegg, J., & Pegg, S. (2015). Razed, repressed, and bought off: The demobilization of the Ogoni protest campaign in the Niger Delta. *The Extractive Industries and Society*, *2*(4), 654–663.

Dibua, J. I. (2004). Conflict over control of natural resources in Nigeria: The case of the oil-producing Niger Delta communities of the South-South States, 1990–2004. *Lagos Historical Review, 4*, 142–172.

Dike, K. O. (1956). *Trade and Politics in the Niger Delta 1830–1885: An Introduction to the Economic and Political History of Nigeria*. Oxford, UK: Oxford University Press.

Dokpesi, A. O., & Ibiezugbe, M. I. (2012). Assessing the human development efforts of the Niger Delta Development Commission. In O. Ukaga, U. O. Ukiwo, & I. S. Ibiba (eds.), *Natural Resources, conflict, and Sustainable Development: Lessons from the Niger Delta* (pp. 60–78). New York, NY: Routledge.

Don-Pedro, Ibiba. (2001, January 18). Natural resources and imperative of state control. The *Guardian Newspaper*, p. 15

Dudley, B. (1982). *An Introduction to Nigerian Government and Politics*. Ibadan, Nigeria: Macmillan Publishers.

Edame, G. E., & Effiong, C. E. (2013). The trend analysis of oil revenue and export in Nigeria. *Journal of Business and Management*, *10*(3), 1–8.

Ejobowah, J. B. (2000). Who owns the oil? The politics of ethnicity in the Niger Delta of Nigeria. *Africa Today*, *47*(1), 29–47.

Ezeilo, N. (2007). Amazons go to war without weapons: Women and the conflict in Escravos, Niger Delta, Nigeria. In I. O. Albert (ed.), *Local approaches to Conflict Transformation* (pp. 65–75). Ibadan, Nigeria: CEPACS.

Frynas, J. G. (2001). Corporate and state responses to anti-oil protests in the Niger Delta. *African Affairs*, *100*(398), 27–54.

Fund for Peace. (2016, July 31). New wave of militancy in the Niger Delta, a joint report by The Fund for Peace, Partnerships Initiative in the Niger Delta and the Niger Delta Partnership Initiative. Retrieved from https://www.ndpifoundation.org/wp-content/uploads/2018/09/Briefing_New-Wave-of-Militancy-in-the-Niger-Delta.pd

Fund for Peace. (2016). Niger Delta Quarterly Conflict Trends, July–September. https://reliefweb.int/report/niger/niger-delta-quarterly-conflict-trends-july-september-2016

Goertz, G., & Diehl, P. F. (1993). Enduring rivalries: Theoretical constructs and empirical patterns. *International Studies Quarterly, 37*(2), 147–171.

Hassan, A. (2013). Review of the global oil and gas industry: a concise journey from ancient times to modern world. *Petroleum Technology Development, 3*(2), 138–160.

Human Rights Watch. (1995). *Nigeria, The Ogoni Crisis: A Case-Study of Military Repression in Southeastern Nigeria*. New York, NY: Human Rights Watch.

Human Rights Watch. (2005). *Rivers and blood: Guns, oil and power in Nigeria's Rivers State*. New York: Human Rights Watch.

Ibeanu, O. (2000). Oiling the friction: Environmental conflict management in the Niger Delta, Nigeria. *Environmental Change and Security Report*, 6, 19–32.

Ihonvbere, J. (2009. Report of the technical committee on the Niger Delta. Retrieved from https://julius.ihonvbere.com/report-of-the-technical-committee-on-the-niger-delta/

Ikelegbe, A. (2001). Civil Society, oil and conflict in the Niger Delta region of Nigeria: ramifications of civil society for a regional resource struggle. *Journal of Modern African Studies, 39*(3), 437–469.

Ikelegbe, A. (2010). *Oil, Resource Conflicts, and the Post Conflict Transition in the Niger Delta region: Beyond the Amnesty*. Center for Population and Environmental Development (CPED) Monograph Series, No.3, Benin City, Nigeria.

International Crisis Group. (2006). *The Swamps of Insurgency: Nigeria's Delta Unrest*. Brussels, Belgium: International Crisis Group.

Isumonah, V. A. (2015). Minority mobilization in the struggle for resource control in Nigeria. *The Extractive Industries and Society, 2*(4), 645–653.

Khan, S. A. (1994). *Nigeria: The Political Economy of Oil*. Oxford, UK: Oxford University Press.

Kriesberg, L., & Dayton, B. W. (2012). *Constructive conflicts: From Escalation to resolution*. Lanham, MD: Rowman & Littlefield Publishers.

Kumolu, C. (2017, July 9). Restructure Nigeria now or no oil bloc, election in 2019 - Niger Delta Group. *Vanguard Newspaper,* Nigeria. Retrieved from https://www.vanguardngr.com/2017/07/restructure-nigeria-now-or-no-oil-bloc-election-in-2019-niger-delta-group/

Lewicki, R. J., Barry, B., & Saunders, D. M. (2010). *Negotiation*. New York, NY: McGraw-Hill Irwin.

Manby, B. (1999). *The price of oil: Corporate responsibility and Human Rights Violations in Nigeria's Oil-Producing Communities*. New York: Human Rights Watch.

Mo Ibrahim Foundation. (2018). Publishes the Annual Ibrahim Index of Governance. Retrieved from http://mo.ibrahim.foundation/iiag/

Moruku, R. K. (2012). The state, multinational oil companies, and restiveness in the Niger Delta: towards a holistic crisis management. *Journal of Alternative Perspectives in Social Sciences, 3*(4), 883–913.

Movement for the Survival of the Ogoni People. (2001, January 26). Presentation of MOSOP to the Judicial Commission for the Investigation of Human Rights Violations aka Justice Oputa Panel Sitting in Port Harcourt Rivers State, Nigeria.

Movement for the Survival of the Ogoni People (MOSOP-USA). (2006). *Annual Report*. Chicago, IL: Vincent Idemyor.

Murphy, H. (2019, March 15). Colombia's Cano Limon pipeline bombed for the 12th time in 2019. *Reuters*. Retrieved from https://www.reuters.com/article/us-colombia-pipeline/colombias-cano-limon-pipeline-bombed-for-12th-time-in-2019-idUSKCN1QW2YX

Ndujihe, C. (2016, August 21). #96 Trillion oil revenue: How Nigeria short-changed oil producing areas. *Vanguard Newspaper*. Retrieved from https://www.vanguardngr.com/2016/08/n96-trillion-oil-revenue-nigeria-short-changed-oil-producing-areas/

Nigeria Extractive Industries Transparency Initiative (NEITI) (2017, February 15). Solid Mineral Report 2015. Retrieved from http://neiti.gov.ng/

NigeriaWatch. (2006). This database aims to compile and monitor homicides and violent deaths (including accidents) in Nigeria in order to provide statistics, analyze trends and draw maps that can help to localize dangerous spots and secure transport of passengers and goods. Retrieved from http://nigeriawatch.org/

Nnoli, O. (1980). *Ethnic Politics in Nigeria*. Enugu, Nigeria: Fourth Dimension Publishers.

Obasi, I. N., & Otobo, E. E. (2011). Selected country study: Nigeria. In L. Adamolekun (ed.), *Public Administration in Africa: Main Issues and Selected Countries Studies* (pp. 413–442). Ibadan, Nigeria: Evans Brothers Publishers.

Obi, C. (2012). Because of oil? Understanding the globalization of the Niger Delta and its consequences. In O. Ukaga, U. Ukiwo, & I. S. Ibaba (eds.), *Natural resources, conflict, and Sustainable Development* (pp. 22–28). New York, NY: Routledge.

Ojo, E. O. (2010). The politics of revenue allocation and resource control in Nigeria: Implications for federal stability. *Federal Governance*, *7*(1), 15–38.

Okonta, I. (2008). *When Citizens Revolt: Nigerian Elites, Big Oil and the Ogoni Struggle for Self-Determination*. Trenton, NJ: Africa World Press.

Okonta, I., & Douglas, O. (2001). *Where Vultures Feast; Shell, Human Rights and Oil in the Niger Delta*. San Francisco, CA: Sierra Club Books.

Oladesu, E. (2009, August 10). The Niger Delta: Path to Peace. *The Nation Newspaper*, Nigeria, p. 13.

Omeje, K. (2005). Oil conflict in Nigeria: Contending issues and perspectives of the local Niger Delta people. *New Political Economy*, *10*(3), 321–334.

Omotola, J. S. (2009). Dissent and State excesses in the Niger Delta, Nigeria. *Studies in Conflict & Terrorism*, *32*(2), 129–145.

Omotoso, F. (2010). Nigerian Fiscal federalism and revenue allocation formula for sustainable development in Niger Delta. *The Social Sciences*, *5*(3), 246–253.

Organization of Petroleum Exporting Countries (OPEC) 2018. Member Countries. Facts and Figures Retrieved from https://www.opec.org/opec_web/en/

Orogun, P. S. (2010). Resource control, revenue allocation, and petroleum politics in Nigeria: the Niger Delta question. *GeoJournal*, *75*(5), 459–507.

Osaghae, E. E. (2008). Social movements and rights claims: the case of action groups in the Niger Delta of Nigeria. *Voluntas*, *19*(2), 189–210.

Pearce, W. B., & Littlejohn, S. W. (1997). *Moral conflict: When Social Worlds Collide*. Thousand Oaks, CA: Sage.

Pegg, S. (1999). The Cost of doing business: Transnational corporations and violence in Nigeria. *Security Dialogue, 30*(4), 473–484.

Post, K. W. J. (1963). *The Nigerian Federal Elections* of 1959. *Politics and Administration in a Developing Political System*. London, UK: Oxford University Press.

Rivers State of Nigeria. (1991). *Judicial Commission of Inquiry into Umuechem Disturbances under the Chairmanship of Hon. Justice Opubo Inko-Tariah*. Rivers State of Nigeria, Port Harcourt.

Sagay, I. (2001, May 21). Nigeria: Federalism, the constitution, and resource control. The *Guardian Newspaper*, Nigeria, pp. 30–31.

Saro-Wiwa, K. (1989). *On A Darkling Plain: An Account of the Nigerian Civil War*. Lagos, Nigeria: Saros International Publishers.

Saro-Wiwa, K. (1992). *Genocide in Nigeria: The Ogoni Tragedy*. Lagos, Nigeria: Saros International Publishers.

Saro-Wiwa, K. (1995). *A Month and A Day: A Detention Diary*. London, UK: Penguin Books.

Senewo, I. (2015). The Ogoni bill of rights; extent of actualization 25 years later? *The Extractive Industries and Society*, *2*(4), 664–670.

Sites, P. (1973). *Control: The basis of Social Order*. New York, NY: Dunellen.

Steers, R. M. (1984). *Introduction to Organizational Behavior*. Glenview, IL: Scott Foresman.

Suberu, R. (2010). The Nigerian federal system: Performance, problems and prospects. *Journal of Contemporary African Studies, 28*(4), 459–477.

Sukubo, I. (2018, February 6). For 40 years, SPDC devastated our kingdom, Rivers monarch, residents cry out, *Vanguard Newspaper*, Nigeria. Retrieved from https://www.vanguardngr.com/2018/02/40-yrs-spdc-devastated-kingdom-rivers-monarch-residents-cry/

Ukaga, O., Ukiwo, U.O., & Ibiba, I. S. (eds.). (2012). *Natural resources, conflict and Sustainable Development: lessons from the Niger Delta*. New York, NY: Routledge.

Ukiwo, U. (2007). From "pirates" to "militants": a historical perspective on anti-state and anti-oil company mobilization among the Ijaw of Warri, Western Niger Delta. *African Affairs*, *106*(425), 587–610.

Umejesi, I. (2012). The Nation State, resource conflict, and the challenges of "former sovereignties" in Nigeria. *African Studies Quarterly, 13*(3), 47–66.

Umukoro, N. (2012). Governance and environmental inequity in Nigeria: implications for conflict management strategies in the Niger Delta. *International Journal of Environmental Studies, 69*(6), 913–920.

United Nations. (1996). Report of the United Nations Secretary General's Fact-Finding Mission to Nigeria, United Nations, New York. Retrieved from https://www.un.org/documents/ga/docs/51/plenary/a51-538.htm

United Nations Environment Program. (2011). Environmental Assessment of Ogoniland, United Environment Program, Nairobi, Kenya.

United Nations Development Program Nigeria. (2006). *Niger Delta Human Development Report.* Abuja, Nigeria: UNDP.

Waidor-Prebagha, S. (1993, April 18). Ogoni Day of Protests. *Newswatch, Cover Story, 65*, 10–14.

Watts, M. J. (2009). Crude politics: Life and death on the Nigerian oil fields (Working paper no. 25). In *Niger Delta: Economies of Violence* (pp. 1–27). Institute of International Studies, University of California, Berkeley, CA: The United States Institute of Peace.

Watts, M. J. (2015). Control of a future foretold: The complex legacies of Ken Saro-Wiwa. *The Extractive Industries and Society*, *2*(4), 635–644.

Williams, P. D. (2011). *War and Conflict in Africa*, Malden, MA: Polity Press.

Wolpe, H. (1974). *Urban Politics in Nigeria: A Study of Port Harcourt.* Berkeley, CA: University of California Press.

World Population Review. (2019). The population of Port Harcourt, Rivers State, Nigeria. Retrieved from http://worldpopulationreview.com/countries/nigeria-population/cities/

Index

About the Author

John B. Idamkue worked as a young community organizer in Ogoni area of the Niger Delta in the 1990s and helped Ken Saro-Wiwa organize the 1993 peaceful march where 300,000 people protested the environmental practices of oil corporations and called for a fair share in the gas resources found in their territory. During 1993–1997, he did advocacy work internationally for the Movement for the Survival of the Ogoni People (MOSOP) and utilized international procedures at the United Nations Human Rights Commission, Geneva, United Nations Working Group on Indigenous Peoples, and the United Nations Committee on the Elimination of Racial Discrimination (CERD). He served as leader of an eight-member MOSOP delegation that received the 1994 Right Livelihood Award given to Ken Saro-Wiwa and MOSOP in the Swedish Parliament in December 1994.

www.ingramcontent.com/pod-product-compliance
Ingram Content Group UK Ltd.
Pitfield, Milton Keynes, MK11 3LW, UK
UKHW041937031026
476234UK00002B/16

9 781793 634801